U.S. Department of Justice
Office of Justice Programs
National Institute of Justice

I0476890

National Institute of Justice

Law Enforcement and Corrections Standards and Testing Program

**Flammable and Combustible Liquid
Spill/Burn Patterns**

NIJ Report 604–00

ABOUT THE LAW ENFORCEMENT AND CORRECTIONS STANDARDS AND TESTING PROGRAM

The Law Enforcement and Corrections Standards and Testing Program is sponsored by the Office of Science and Technology of the National Institute of Justice (NIJ), U.S. Department of Justice. The program responds to the mandate of the Justice System Improvement Act of 1979, which directed NIJ to encourage research and development to improve the criminal justice system and to disseminate the results to Federal, State, and local agencies.

The Law Enforcement and Corrections Standards and Testing Program is an applied research effort that determines the technological needs of justice system agencies, sets minimum performance standards for specific devices, tests commercially available equipment against those standards, and disseminates the standards and the test results to criminal justice agencies nationally and internationally.

The program operates through:

The *Law Enforcement and Corrections Technology Advisory Council* (LECTAC), consisting of nationally recognized criminal justice practitioners from Federal, State, and local agencies, which assesses technological needs and sets priorities for research programs and items to be evaluated and tested.

The *Office of Law Enforcement Standards* (OLES) at the National Institute of Standards and Technology, which develops voluntary national performance standards for compliance testing to ensure that individual items of equipment are suitable for use by criminal justice agencies. The standards are based upon laboratory testing and evaluation of representative samples of each item of equipment to determine the key attributes, develop test methods, and establish minimum performance requirements for each essential attribute. In addition to the highly technical standards, OLES also produces technical reports and user guidelines that explain in nontechnical terms the capabilities of available equipment.

The *National Law Enforcement and Corrections Technology Center (NLECTC),* operated by a grantee, which supervises a national compliance testing program conducted by independent laboratories. The standards developed by OLES serve as performance benchmarks against which commercial equipment is measured. The facilities, personnel, and testing capabilities of the independent laboratories are evaluated by OLES prior to testing each item of equipment, and OLES helps the NLECTC staff review and analyze data. Test results are published in Equipment Performance Reports designed to help justice system procurement officials make informed purchasing decisions.

Publications are available at no charge through the National Law Enforcement and Corrections Technology Center. Some documents are also available online through the Internet/World Wide Web. To request a document or additional information, call 800–248–2742 or 301–519–5060, or write:

National Law Enforcement and Corrections Technology Center
P.O. Box 1160
Rockville, MD 20849–1160
E-Mail: *asknlectc@nlectc.org*
World Wide Web address: *http://www.nlectc.org*

The National Institute of Justice is a component of the Office of Justice Programs, which also includes the Bureau of Justice Assistance, the Bureau of Justice Statistics, the Office of Juvenile Justice and Delinquency Prevention, and the Office for Victims of Crime.

U.S. Department of Justice
Office of Justice Programs
National Institute of Justice

Flammable and Combustible Liquid Spill/Burn Patterns

NIJ Report 604–00

Anthony D. Putorti, Jr.
Fire Safety Engineering Division
Building and Fire Research Laboratory
National Institute of Standards and Technology
Gaithersburg, MD 20899–8641

Prepared for:
National Institute of Justice
Office of Science and Technology
Washington, DC 20531

March 2001

NCJ 186634

National Institute of Justice

The technical effort to develop this report was conducted
under Interagency Agreement 94–IJ–R–004,
Project No. 96–002.
This report was prepared with the assistance
of the Office of Law Enforcement
Standards (OLES) of the National Institute of Standards
and Technology (NIST) under the direction of
Kathleen M. Higgins, Director of OLES.
The work resulting from this report was sponsored by the
National Institute of Justice (NIJ), Dr. David G. Boyd, Director,
Office of Science and Technology.

FOREWORD

The Office of Law Enforcement Standards (OLES) of the National Institute of Standards and Technology (NIST) furnishes technical support to the National Institute of Justice (NIJ) program to strengthen law enforcement and criminal justice in the United States. OLES's function is to conduct research that will assist law enforcement and criminal justice agencies in the selection and procurement of quality equipment.

OLES is: (1) Subjecting existing equipment to laboratory testing and evaluation, and (2) conducting research leading to the development of several series of documents, including national standards, user guides, and technical reports.

This document covers research conducted by OLES under the sponsorship of the National Institute of Justice. Additional reports as well as other documents are being issued under the OLES program in the areas of protective clothing and equipment, communications systems, emergency equipment, investigative aids, security systems, vehicles, weapons, and analytical techniques and standard reference materials used by the forensic community.

Technical comments and suggestions concerning this report are invited from all interested parties. They may be addressed to the Office of Law Enforcement Standards, National Institute of Standards and Technology, 100 Bureau Drive, Stop 8102, Gaithersburg, MD 20899–8102.

Dr. David G. Boyd, Director
Office of Science and Technology
National Institute of Justice

CONTENTS

TABLES

FIGURES

COMMONLY USED SYMBOLS AND ABBREVIATIONS

A	ampere	H	henry	nm	nanometer
ac	alternating current	h	hour	No.	number
AM	amplitude modulation	hf	high frequency	o.d.	outside diameter
cd	candela	Hz	hertz	Ω	ohm
cm	centimeter	i.d.	inside diameter	p.	page
CP	chemically pure	in	inch	Pa	pascal
c/s	cycle per second	IR	infrared	pe	probable error
d	day	J	joule	pp.	pages
dB	decibel	L	lambert	ppm	parts per million
dc	direct current	L	liter	qt	quart
°C	degree Celsius	lb	pound	rad	radian
°F	degree Fahrenheit	lbf	pound-force	rf	radio frequency
dia	diameter	lbf·in	pound-force inch	rh	relative humidity
emf	electromotive force	lm	lumen	s	second
eq	equation	ln	logarithm (base e)	SD	standard deviation
F	farad	log	logarithm (base 10)	sec.	section
fc	footcandle	M	molar	SWR	standing wave ratio
fig.	figure	m	meter	uhf	ultrahigh frequency
FM	frequency modulation	min	minute	UV	ultraviolet
ft	foot	mm	millimeter	V	volt
ft/s	foot per second	mph	miles per hour	vhf	very high frequency
g	acceleration	m/s	meter per second	W	watt
g	gram	N	newton	λ	wavelength
gr	grain	N·m	newton meter	wt	weight

area=unit^2 (e.g., ft^2, in^2, etc.); volume=unit^3 (e.g., ft^3, m^3, etc.)

PREFIXES

d	deci (10^{-1})	da	deka (10)
c	centi (10^{-2})	h	hecto (10^2)
m	milli (10^{-3})	k	kilo (10^3)
μ	micro (10^{-6})	M	mega (10^6)
n	nano (10^{-9})	G	giga (10^9)
p	pico (10^{-12})	T	tera (10^{12})

COMMON CONVERSIONS
(See ASTM E380)

0.30480 m =1ft	4.448222 N = 1 lbf
2.54 cm = 1 in	1.355818 J =1 ft·lbf
0.4535924 kg = 1 lb	0.1129848 N m = 1 lbf·in
0.06479891g = 1gr	14.59390 N/m =1 lbf/ft
0.9463529 L = 1 qt	6894.757 Pa = 1 lbf/in^2
3600000 J = 1 kW·hr	1.609344 km/h = 1 mph

Temperature: $T_C = (T_F - 32) \times 5/9$

Temperature: $T_F = (T_C \times 9/5) + 32$

NIJ Report 604–00

FLAMMABLE AND COMBUSTIBLE LIQUID SPILL/BURN PATTERNS

Anthony D. Putorti Jr.
Jay A. McElroy
Daniel Madrzykowski

Fire Safety Engineering Division, Building and Fire Research Laboratory
National Institute of Standards and Technology, Gaithersburg, MD 20899–8641

Discussions with fire investigators indicate that it would be beneficial to have the ability to predict the quantity of liquid fuel necessary to create a burn pattern of a given size. Full-scale spill and fire experiments were conducted with gasoline and kerosene on vinyl, wood parquet, and carpet covered plywood floors using various quantities of fuel. Spill areas were measured, and for nonporous floors the results were compared to analytical predictions. Burn pattern areas are correlated with the spill areas, resulting in a method for predicting the quantity of spilled fuel required to form a burn pattern of a given size. The heat release rates of the fuel spill fires were determined through experiment and compared to an existing reference for burning liquid pools of the same surface area. The peak spill fire heat release rates for nonporous surfaces were found to be approximately 1/8 to 1/4 of those from equivalent area pool fires. The peak heat release rates for spill fires on carpet were found to be approximately equal to those from equivalent area pool fires. The heat release rates can be used as inputs for fire modeling or for evaluating fire scenarios.

Key words: accelerants; arson; building fires; burn patterns; carpets; char; charring; fire investigations; fire measurements; flammable liquids; floors; floor coverings; heat release rate; pour patterns; spill fires.

1. INTRODUCTION

Discussions with fire investigators indicate that it would be beneficial to have the ability to predict the quantity of liquid fuel necessary to create a burn pattern of a given size. Past studies conducted with liquid fuels contained too many variables to determine the relationship between spill quantity and burn pattern area. In an effort to reduce the variables involved, and thereby understand the process of pattern formation, experiments are conducted in the laboratory under an instrumented exhaust hood, without a room or enclosure. This layout would represent a fire burning in a large space, or in an enclosure before the formation of a significant upper layer of heated combustion products. Due to the rapid combustion of fuel spills on nonporous surfaces, the results of the study may be applicable to many enclosures.

Analytical predictions and empirical data concerning the spread of liquids on ideal surfaces are available in the literature. The analytical predictions are based on perfectly smooth, level, and nonporous surfaces. The empirical data is derived from spills on very smooth level surfaces, such as epoxy-coated concrete and metal.

The floor materials of interest to fire investigators, such as wood and vinyl flooring, carpet, and unsealed concrete differ from the ideal surfaces assumed in the analytical predictions. These flooring materials contain joints and texture, and may be porous or semiporous. The spread of liquids on these surfaces is expected to differ from those measured or predicted on more ideal surfaces. This study investigates the spill and burning behavior of liquid fuels on vinyl tile, wood parquet, and carpet flooring materials. In order to provide inputs for fire modeling that can be especially useful in fire condition prediction and fire scenario evaluation, the heat release rates (HRRs) of the spill fires are measured. The liquid fuels used are gasoline and kerosene, which are commonly encountered by fire investigators in the field.

2. ANALYTICAL SPILL SIZE PREDICTION

The literature [1] contains methods for predicting the spread of fluids on smooth, level surfaces. The methods consist of fluid mechanics models that assume a smooth, level surface and negligible evaporation. This assumption will be an approximation in the case of wood and vinyl floors due to surface texture, cracks, and the inability to produce a perfectly smooth, level surface. The analysis is not applicable to carpeted surfaces due to absorption into the carpet and pad.

Properties of the spreading fuel are important to the spreading process. Characteristics such as fuel density, viscosity, surface tension, and the interfacial tension between the liquid, the air, and the floor surface all affect the spreading process.

When a liquid is spilled on a surface, a condition that is assumed to occur instantaneously in the analytical predictions, the spreading process may be divided into a series of three regimes, each of which is dominated by different physical forces. The regimes occur in the following order: gravity-inertia, gravity-viscous, and viscous-surface tension. In the gravity-inertia regime, the forces of gravity are working to spread the fluid and are opposed by the inertia of the fluid. In the gravity-viscous regime, the viscous forces within the fluid oppose the gravity forces. Finally, in the viscous-surface tension regime, the viscous forces within the fluid oppose the surface tension forces. For the fuels and spill sizes investigated here, the spill enters the viscous-surface tension regime very rapidly, on the order of a few seconds from the time of the spill. The process for calculating the spill thickness as a function of time differs depending on the spill regime at the time of interest. Equation 1 is used to determine the time at which the spill enters the viscous-surface tension regime. For $t > t_2$, the spill is in the viscous-surface tension regime, and equation 2 may be used to calculate the radius of the spill and derive the spill thickness.

---

[1] Numbers in brackets refer to references in section 7.

$$t_2 = 0.1697 \left[\frac{GV\mu_l^2}{\sigma v_l} \right]$$

(1)

Where: t_2 • boundary time between the gravity-viscous and viscous-surface
            tension regime(s)
          G • acceleration of gravity (9.81 m/s^2)
          V • spill volume (m^3)
          $\bullet_l$ • absolute viscosity (N s/m^2)
          • • Interfacial tension (N/m)
          $\bullet_l$ • kinematic viscosity (m^2/s)

$$R(t) = 1.05 \left[\frac{\sigma V}{\mu_l} \right]^{\frac{1}{4}} t^{\frac{1}{4}}$$

(2)

Where: R • radius of spill (m)
          T • time (s)

The spill area was predicted as a function of time according to eq (1) and eq (2), using the properties [2] listed in table 1. The results for two times of interest are listed in table 2.

Table 1. Physical properties of spilled fuels

Properties	Gasoline	Kerosene
• (N/m)	2.12×10^{-2}	2.77×10^{-2}
$\bullet_1$ (m^2/s)	4.29×10^{-7}	2.39×10^{-6}
$\bullet_1$ (N s/m^2)	2.92×10^{-4}	1.92×10^{-3}

Table 2. Spill thickness predictions

Fuel	Predicted Thickness, mm (in)	
	60 s	*120 s*
Gasoline	0.56 (0.022)	0.41 (0.016)
Kerosene	1.3 (0.050)	0.89 (0.035)

The spreading of liquid fuels in industrial facilities has been studied for fire hazard analyses [3]. In these experiments, spill thickness of 0.22 mm resulted from unconfined spills of #2 fuel oil on epoxy-coated concrete and steel surfaces. The study found that the unconfined spill thickness was independent of the spill volume, a result that is applied in the current study.

3. SPILL AREA

A series of eight spill area measurements were conducted using wood parquet and vinyl flooring. Various quantities of fuel were poured onto sections of flooring. The flooring sections consisted of a wood frame constructed of 50 mm by 100 mm (2 in x 4 in) nominal wood lumber covered with 16 mm (5/8 in) nominal plywood secured with nails. The wood parquet flooring sections were constructed by applying adhesive to the plywood surface and attaching the 300 mm by 300 mm (12 in by 12 in) nominal wood parquet flooring tiles to the flooring sections. The wood tiles are coated with a clear polyurethane finish at the factory and are manufactured with tongue and groove connections along the tile perimeter. The vinyl flooring sections were constructed by attaching a 6 mm (1/4 in) nominal layer of dense fiberboard to the plywood surface with nails. Self-sticking 300 mm by 300 mm (12 in by 12 in) nominal vinyl flooring tiles were applied to the surface of the fiberboard.

The liquid fuels were poured in the center of the flooring sections, with approximate dimensions of 1.22 m by 1.22 m (4 ft x 4 ft), using the apparatus shown in figure 1. The fuel was poured by rotating the container, thereby discharging the fuel onto the center of the floor sample from a height of 510 mm ± 10 mm. (This estimated expanded uncertainty is the result of a Type B evaluation with a coverage factor of 2.) The fuel was allowed to spread and sit on the surface of the flooring for a duration of approximately 60 s. In all cases, the fuel was observed to have stopped spreading within the 60 s time period. The temperatures of the floor samples and fuel were approximately equal to the ambient temperature, which was approximately 24 °C (75 °F).

Spill areas were measured using infrared imaging. The use of infrared imaging was made possible by emissivity differences between the flooring materials and the fuels, which were at approximately the same temperature. This avoided the need to add dyes or other impurities to the fuels to make them visible. The nominal thickness of the spill was calculated from the spill area and spill quantity. Fuel evaporation and soak-in were ignored due to the short duration of the measurements and the use of nonporous surfaces. Figures 2 and 3 show the extent of the spread of gasoline on wood parquet and vinyl tile floors. The fluid traveling within the cracks of the flooring material can be clearly seen along the periphery of the wood parquet floor spill. The presence of these fuel dendrites was ignored in the calculation of spill thickness.

Spill thicknesses calculated using the analytical method are compared to the experimental results in table 3. All of the uncertainties stated in this report, unless otherwise noted, are expanded uncertainties derived from Type A evaluations (statistical analysis of the data) with a coverage factor, k, equal to 2. A coverage factor of 2 corresponds to a confidence interval of approximately 95 %, assuming a normal distribution applies [4].

Due to the assumptions made in the analytical predictions, most importantly the ideal surface, the spreading behavior of the spill is a function of time. While the spreading in the experiments appeared to cease in less than 60 s, the analytical predictions using eq (1) and eq (2) indicate continual spread. Due to the differences in the analytically predicted and empirical spill thicknesses for the floor coverings studied, the use of the empirical data is recommended. The analytical prediction method is useful, however, for understanding the spreading mechanisms of a fluid spill. The predictions could be valuable for instances where the spill method, fuels, or floor surfaces differ from those studied in this paper. To this end, the analytical prediction method could be used to understand the sensitivity of the spill thickness to variables such as fuel temperature, floor temperature, fuel variations, etc.

Table 3. Comparison of predicted and empirically derived spill thickness

Fuel/Floor Material	Predicted Thickness, mm (in)		Empirically Derived Thickness, mm (in)
	60 s	120 s	
Gasoline/Wood	0.56 (0.022)	0.41 (0.016)	0.67 • 0.05 (0.026 • 0.002)
Gasoline/Vinyl	0.56 (0.022)	0.41 (0.016)	0.56 • 0.05 (0.022 • 0.002)
Kerosene/Wood	1.3 (0.050)	0.89 (0.035)	0.82 • 0.05 (0.032 • 0.002)
Kerosene/Vinyl	1.3 (0.050)	0.89 (0.035)	0.79 • 0.05 (0.031 • 0.002)

Spill areas were also measured on carpeted floors. In this case, the edge of the spill was indicated on the carpet with a black permanent marker, and the dimensions of the elliptical spill measured with a meter stick. Two types of carpet were used. Carpet "1" was composed of polyolefin, with polypropylene backing. This carpet is designated as a home/office carpet, with dense loop construction, and an approximate mass per unit area of 0.68 kg/m^2 (20 oz/yd^2). Carpet "2" was a cut pile carpet composed of nylon, with an approximate mass per unit area of

0.85 kg/m^2 (25 oz/yd^2). Both carpet types were installed over polyurethane carpet padding, with an approximate mass per unit area of 0.98 kg/m^2 (29 oz/yd^2), and attached to a plywood sub-floor with tack strips along the perimeter. Descriptions of the carpets and padding are summarized in table 4.

Table 4. Carpet flooring composition

Carpet Flooring Component	Description
Carpet 1	Home/office carpet with dense loop construction. Polyolefin loops and polypropylene backing. Approximate mass per unit area of 0.68 kg/m^2.
Carpet 2	Cut pile nylon carpet. Approximate mass per unit area of 0.85 kg/m^2.
Padding	Polyurethane foam pad constructed from shredded foam. Approximate mass per unit area of 0.98 kg/m^2. Pad thickness approximately 10 mm.

The carpet spills were conducted in an identical manner to those on the nonporous surfaces, except for the area measurement method stated above, and that a 2.44 m x 2.44 m section of flooring was used for all of the spills. Since the carpet and pad absorb the spilled gasoline, the spill areas for various quantities of fuel are listed in units of area instead of length (thickness). The results are shown in table 5.

Table 5. Carpet spill areas

Carpet Type	Spill Quantity mL (gal.)	Spill Area, m^2 (sq. ft.)
1	250 (0.066)	$8.51 \times 10^{-2} \pm 0.00$ (0.916 $\pm$ 0.00)[*]
1	500 (0.13)	$1.63 \times 10^{-1} \pm 3.33 \times 10^{-2}$ (1.76 $\pm$ 0.359)
1	1000 (0.26)	$2.89 \times 10^{-1} \pm 1.49 \times 10^{-2}$ (3.11 $\pm$ 0.161)
2	250 (0.066)	$3.95 \times 10^{-2} \pm 1.05 \times 10^{-2}$ (0.425 $\pm$ 0.113)
2	500 (0.13)	$5.95 \times 10^{-2} \pm 6.44 \times 10^{-3}$ (0.640 $\pm$ 6.93 $\times 10^{-2}$)
2	1000 (0.26)	$1.07 \times 10^{-1} \pm 1.20 \times 10^{-2}$ (1.15 $\pm$ 0.129)

[*] An estimated expanded uncertainty of $\pm 5.37 \times 10^{-3}$ m^2 ($\pm 5.79 \times 10^{-2}$ ft^2) results from application of the law of propagation of uncertainty to Type B uncertainties using a coverage factor of 2.

4. SPILL IGNITION EXPERIMENTS

The full-scale fire experiments were conducted under an instrumented exhaust hood in the laboratory. The laboratory space is temperature controlled and for all experiments was approximately 20 °C (68 °F). The fuel was poured over the center of each 2.44 m by 2.44 m (8.00 ft x 8.00 ft) nominal flooring section by rotating the vessel to the horizontal. Upon completion of the pour, a soak-in time of approximately 60 s was observed to allow for the spread of the fuel over the surface. During the soak-in time, an electric match consisting of a nickel-chromium wire run through a book of paper matches, was placed in the center of the spill. The spill was ignited at the end of the soak-in period. The real-time heat release rate of the fire was calculated using oxygen consumption calorimetry during the fire [5]. The nonporous flooring fires were allowed to burn until they self-extinguished. The carpet fires were extinguished at various times after ignition. Following extinguishment, the burn pattern resulting from the fire was measured and photographed. The experimental setup is shown in figures 1 and 4, while the gasoline fire experimental matrix is shown in table 6.

4.1 Nonporous Surfaces

As expected, the ignition and burning behaviors of gasoline and kerosene differed. Gasoline (87 octane), a liquid with a closed cup flashpoint of −38 °C [6], ignited readily and consistently with flame spreading rapidly over the entire surface of the spill (see fig. 5). In addition, vapors spread past the confines of the spill during the soak-in time, resulting in momentary burning over a larger area, which was not measured. Spill fires approaching extinction are shown in figures 6 and 7. In both cases, fire can be seen lingering in the cracks and seams present in the surfaces of the floors.

Figures 8 through 11 show the typical patterns left by the gasoline fires. Upon inspection of the floors after the burns, it was noted that the charring was limited to the upper surface of the flooring and in the cracks of the tiles. In the wood parquet flooring experiments, the plywood underlayment was undamaged. In the vinyl flooring tests, the fiberboard underlayment was undamaged, except for charring at the seams between the tiles. The charring of the fiberboard can be seen in figures 12 and 13 where the tiles pulled away from each other at the seams upon fire exposure.

Kerosene, a liquid with a closed cup flashpoint of 55 °C [7], did not ignite readily or consistently. The kerosene failed to ignite in most cases. In some of the experiments, the kerosene did ignite in the locality of the matches and slowly spread in the confines of cracks in the floor. This behavior led to the pattern shown in figure 14. The kerosene fires self-extinguished leaving large areas of the spill unburned. Given the limited amount of burning from the kerosene, most of the experiments were conducted with gasoline.

Table 6. Gasoline fire experimental matrix

Floor Type	Spill Quantity (mL)	Number of Experiments
Wood Parquet	250	3
Wood Parquet	500	3
Wood Parquet	1000	3
Vinyl	250	3
Vinyl	500	3
Vinyl	1000	4
Carpet 1	250	3
Carpet 1	500	3
Carpet 1	1000	3
Carpet 2	250	3
Carpet 2	500	3
Carpet 2	1000	4

4.2 Carpeted Surfaces

The spill fires on carpeted flooring utilized gasoline (87 octane) as the spilled fuel. As with the nonporous surfaces, the gasoline ignited readily and consistently with flame spreading rapidly over the entire surface of the spill. In addition, vapors spread past the confines of the spill during the soak-in time, resulting in momentary burning over a larger area, which was not measured. The two types of carpet differed qualitatively in the rate of flame spread over the carpet surface. The flame spread rate of the cut pile nylon carpet (carpet 2) was significantly less than that of the polyolefin carpet (carpet 1) of loop construction. The flame spread rates were not characterized quantitatively, but the fire area of the polyolefin carpet experiments more than doubled in 90 s, as opposed to the nylon carpet experiments where the burn area only increased slightly over the same time period. This behavior is illustrated in figures 15 through 18.

Close-up views of the burning carpet spills are shown in figures 19 and 20.

Post-fire, the burn pattern present on the carpeted floors exhibited a "doughnut" type pattern, as can be seen in figures 21 through 24. The presence of gasoline was limited to the inside doughnut, where significant quantities of fuel were present. The melted carpet material inside the doughnut protected the carpet padding from the effects of the fire (fig. 25). The protected carpet pad was soaked with gasoline post-fire, and could be reignited with an open flame. Several of the nylon carpeted fires were allowed to burn for extended periods of time, approximately 1800 s (30 min), until the fire consisted of distributed areas of small individual flames (fig. 26). The protected carpet padding inside the doughnut pattern was soaked with gasoline after the extended burn time. After the fires were extinguished, the carpet and padding could be removed, leaving the doughnut pattern attached to the underlying plywood flooring. This is shown in figure 27.

5. ANALYSIS AND RESULTS

5.1 Spill and Burn Areas

The spill areas and burn areas for the nonporous floors are compared in figures 28 and 29. The error bars on the graphs represent the expanded uncertainty in the measurement of the spill area. The graphs illustrate good agreement between the spill and burn areas for gasoline. The burn areas from the gasoline spill fires on wood and vinyl floors are well represented by a linear curve fit. The y-intercept is positive, suggesting the effects of uncertainty, or that the burn area is slightly larger than the spill area. For wood floors, the latter is illustrated by the comparison of the spill and burn areas. In the case of vinyl, however, the spill and burn areas are essentially the same. Note that for the wood and vinyl surfaces, the spill areas on the graph are extrapolated from the 250 mL spills to the 500 mL and 1000 mL spills. The basis for the extrapolation was previous work in the literature [3] where unconfined spill thicknesses on nonporous surfaces were found to be independent of spill volume. Points are shown at 500 mL and 1000 mL in order to illustrate the uncertainty in the extrapolation, derived from the law of propagation of uncertainty and the uncertainty in the 250 mL result.

The spill and initial burn areas for the carpet experiments, shown in figure 30, are well represented by a linear curve fit. The areas are greater for the low pile looped polyolefin carpet as compared to the cut pile nylon carpet as a consequence of the quantity of fuel the carpet is able to hold. In both cases, the y-intercept is positive due to uncertainties and/or the pouring of the fuel. Since the area of the pour stream is the same for all of the pours, it would compose a greater percentage of the spill area at smaller spill volumes. There is also a small amount of slop and splatter that occurs when the fuel stream contacts the surface of the floor. As the spill volume approaches zero, a minimum spill area would be expected, and the extrapolation would cease to be valid. Note that the spill areas of the porous surfaces are an order of magnitude smaller than those on the nonporous surfaces studied.

5.2 Peak Heat Release Rate

The peak heat release rate versus spill volume relationships for the vinyl and wood flooring are well represented by a linear curve fit, shown in figure 31. Note that the y-intercept for the vinyl flooring is positive; it is the result of uncertainty in the measurement, or possibly it illustrates the contribution of the vinyl flooring material to the heat release rate. In contrast to the vinyl-flooring plot, the linear fit for the wood flooring has a negative y-intercept. This could be the result of uncertainty, or the combined effects of the heat release rate contribution of the flooring and the fluid lost into the cracks of the flooring material.

The peak heat release rate versus spill volume of the carpeted floors, shown in figure 32, are both represented well by a linear fit, with the polyolefin carpet spills having greater rates of heat release than the nylon carpet spills, at the spill sizes examined. This result was expected given the qualitative behavior observed during the experiments, where the polyolefin burns exhibited a greater rate of flame spread than the nylon carpet burns. In both cases, the fit has a positive y-intercept, due to the uncertainty in the data, or to the heat release rate component of the carpet and pad.

The peak heat release rates for the spill fires are compared to steady state pool fire heat release rates in tables 7 and 8. The pool fire HRR values were computed from correlations derived from large-scale pool fire experiments [8,9]. The diameters used in the pool fire HRR correlations are equivalent diameters, i.e., the areas of the pool fires are the same as the areas of the spill fires. Peak heat release rates for the spills examined on nonporous surfaces are approximately 1/4 to 1/8 of the heat release rates of the pool fires. For the carpet spill fires, the peak heat release rates are approximately equal to the steady state heat release rates of the equivalent diameter pool fires. For the scenarios examined, the pool fire heat release rates would not be good approximations for gasoline spills on nonporous surfaces for modeling purposes. The pool fire heat release rates, however, are good approximations for gasoline spill fire heat release rates on the carpeted flooring surfaces examined.

The heat release rates of the fire experiments as a function of time are included in the graphs in appendix A.

Table 7. Nonporous spill fire and pool fire HRR

Spill Volume, mL (gal.)	Peak HRR (kW)		Pool Fire Steady HRR (kW)	
	Wood	Vinyl	Wood	Vinyl
1000 (0.26)	770 ± 120	590 ± 160	3200	3900
500 (0.13)	320 ± 80	310 ± 30	1500	1800
250 (0.066)	110 ± 100[**]	180 ± 80	700	800

[**]If one of the three experiments could be classified as a statistical outlier, the average peak heat release rate would be 80 kW ± 0 kW. Using Chauvenet's Criterion, however, the experimental result is not an outlier assuming a normal probability distribution. See Holman, J.P. *Experimental Methods for Engineers,* McGraw-Hill, New York, 1989.

Table 8. Carpet spill fire and pool fire HRR

Spill Volume, mL (gal.)	Peak HRR (kW)		Pool Fire Steady HRR (kW)	
	Carpet 1	Carpet 2	Carpet 1	Carpet 2
1000 (0.26)	460 ± 30	180 ± 30	470	130
500 (0.13)	230 ± 20	110 ± 0	230	60
250 (0.066)	130 ± 10	60 ± 10	100	40

5.3 Heat Release Rate Per Unit Area

The heat release rate per unit area (HRR/area) is nearly constant for the vinyl flooring spill fires studied, and is shown in figure 33. The wood flooring experiments, however, displayed an increase in the heat release rate per unit area as the spill size increased. Given the overall behavior of the HRR/area for the wood floor spills, and the HRR linear curve fit which has a negative y-intercept, some of the fuel may have been lost into the cracks of the parquet surface. Given the construction of the flooring, it would be expected that more fuel would be lost into the parquet than into the vinyl due to the greater crack length per unit area of the parquet flooring.

The HRR/area for the spills on carpet are shown in figure 34. The spills on polyolefin carpet have a nearly constant HRR/area over the spill size range studied. For the nylon carpet, a linear fit is not a good representation for the HRR/area data. As a comparison, the pool fire HRR/area is nearly constant over the range of equivalent pool fire diameters examined [8]. The resulting pool fires in this range would be in the turbulent flow regime, where radiative feedback effects and turbulent flow effects are important. The reason for the larger HRR/area value resulting from the 500 mL nylon carpet burns should be studied further.

6. CONCLUSIONS

Based on a limited number of experiments, the conclusions of this study can be summarized by the following:

1. The spill area can be predicted from the fuel quantity. The empirically derived spill thickness can be used to predict the size of spills.

2. In all but one scenario, the nonporous flooring gasoline burn areas were found to be the same as the spill areas within the experimental uncertainty.

3. Initial carpet burn areas were found to be the same as the carpet spill areas, within the experimental uncertainty.

4. The quantity of gasoline spilled could be determined from the burn pattern area on nonporous flooring.

5. Significant quantities of spilled fuel were present after extinguishment and extinction of the carpeted fires. The melted carpet inside the doughnut protected the unburned liquid.

6. Peak heat release rates for the spills examined on nonporous surfaces are approximately 1/4 to 1/8 of the heat release rates of equivalent diameter pool fires. For the carpet spill fires, the peak heat release rates are approximately equal to the steady state heat release rates of the equivalent diameter pool fires.

7. Pool fire heat release rates may be useful for fire modeling and fire scenario evaluation for spill fires on carpeted floors. Fire modeling and fire scenario evaluation for spill fires on nonporous floors should not be conducted using the heat release rates derived from pool fires.

This report provides a means for fire investigators to predict the quantity of spilled gasoline necessary to produce a fire pattern of a particular size on various types of commonly used flooring materials. It also includes measurements of spill fire heat release rates that provide fire investigators and other fire professionals with previously unavailable data for fire modeling and fire scenario evaluation.

7. REFERENCES

[1]   P.P.K. Raj and A.S. Kalelkar, *Assessment Models in Support of the Hazard Assessment Handbook*. U.S. Coast Guard Report AD–776 617, U.S. Coast Guard Headquarters, Washington, DC (1974).

[2]   J.W. Murdock, "Mechanics of Fluids." *Marks' Standard Handbook for Mechanical Engineers*. Tenth Edition, E.A. Avallone and T. Baumeister III, eds., McGraw-Hill, New York, NY (1996), pp. 3-31 to 3-33.

[3]   A.T. Modak, "Ignitability of High-Fire-Point Liquid Spills." EPRI Report NP-1731, Electric Power Research Institute, Palo Alto, CA (1981).

[4]   B.N. Taylor and C.E. Kuyatt, "Guidelines for Evaluating and Expressing the Uncertainty of NIST Measurement Results." NIST Technical Note 1297, 1994 Edition, National Institute of Standards and Technology, Gaithersburg, MD 20899.

[5]   V. Babrauskas, R.L. Lawson, W.D. Walton, and W.H. Twilley, "Upholstered Furniture Heat Release Rates Measured With a Furniture Calorimeter." NBSIR 82-2604, National Bureau of Standards, December 1982.

[6]   D. Drysdale, "Ignition: The Initiation of Flaming Combustion." *An Introduction to Fire Dynamics.* John Wiley & Sons Ltd., Reprinted September 1986, p. 197.

[7]   A.M. Kanury, "Ignition of Liquid Fuels." *SFPE Handbook of Fire Protection Engineering,* Second Edition, P.J. DiNenno et al. eds., Society of Fire Protection Engineers, Boston (1995), pp. 2-163.

[8]   K.S. Mudan and P.A. Croce, "Fire Hazard Calculations for Large Open Hydrocarbon Fires." *SFPE Handbook of Fire Protection Engineering,* Second Edition, P.J. DiNenno et. al. eds., Society of Fire Protection Engineers, Boston (1995) pp. 3-199.

[9]   A. Tewarson, "Generation of Heat and Chemical Compounds in Fires." *SFPE Handbook of Fire Protection Engineering,* Second Edition, P.J. DiNenno et al. eds., Society of Fire Protection Engineers (1995), pp. 3-78.

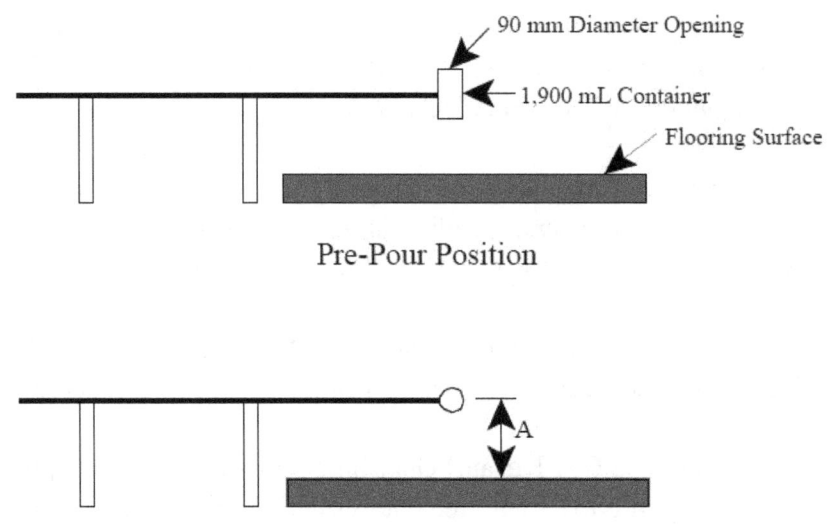

90 mm Diameter Opening

1,900 mL Container

Flooring Surface

Pre-Pour Position

A

Pour Position

Figure 1. *Fuel pour apparatus. The dimension "A" is 510 mm ± 10 mm. The container opening diameter and volume are approximate.*

Figure 2. *Infrared image of gasoline spill on wood parquet floor*

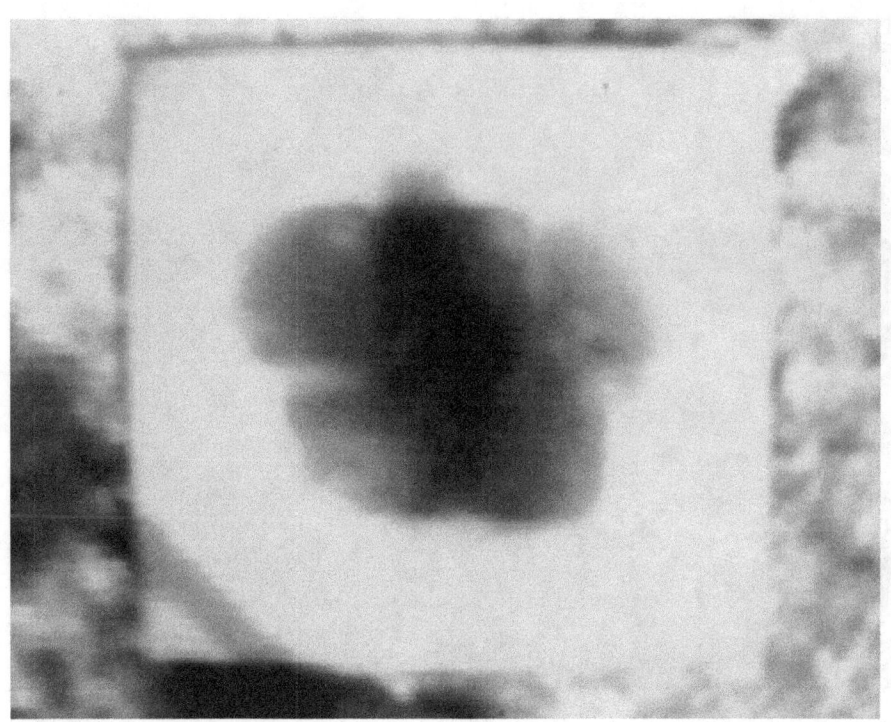

Figure 3. *Infrared image of gasoline spill on vinyl tile floor*

Figure 4. *Gasoline spill fire under the furniture calorimetry hood in the large Fire Research Facility at NIST*

Figure 5. *Ignition of 1,000 mL gasoline spill on wood parquet flooring*

Figure 6. *Burning in the cracks of the parquet flooring*

Figure 7. *Burning in the seams of the vinyl tile flooring*

Figure 8. *1,000 mL gasoline spill fire burn pattern on wood parquet floor*

Figure 9. *Closeup of gasoline spill fire burn pattern on wood parquet floor*

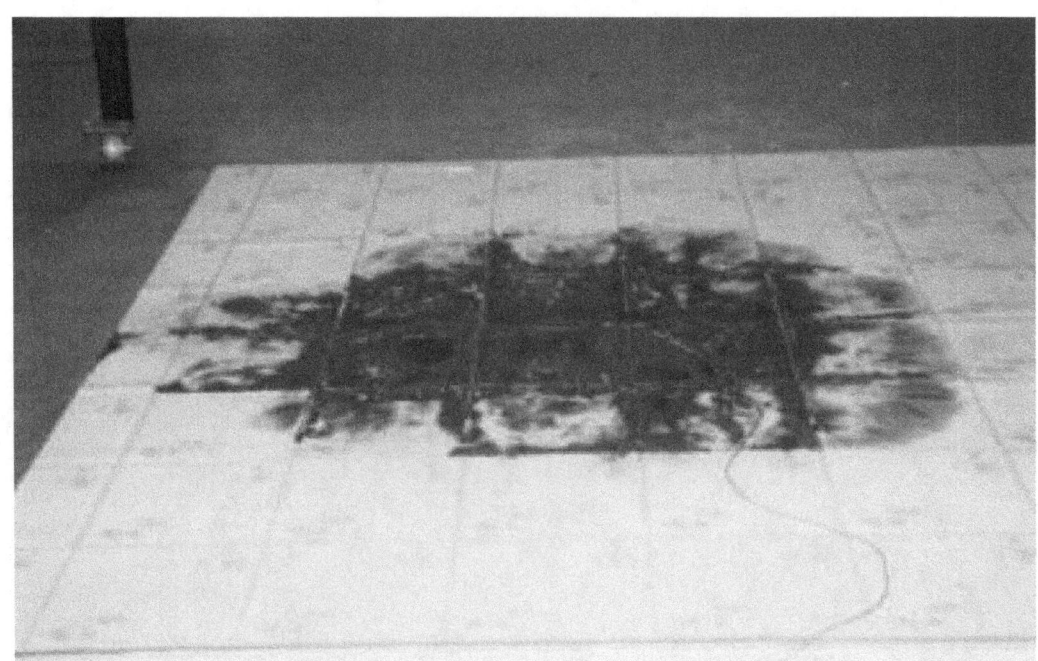

Figure 10. *1,000 mL gasoline spill fire pattern on vinyl tile floor*

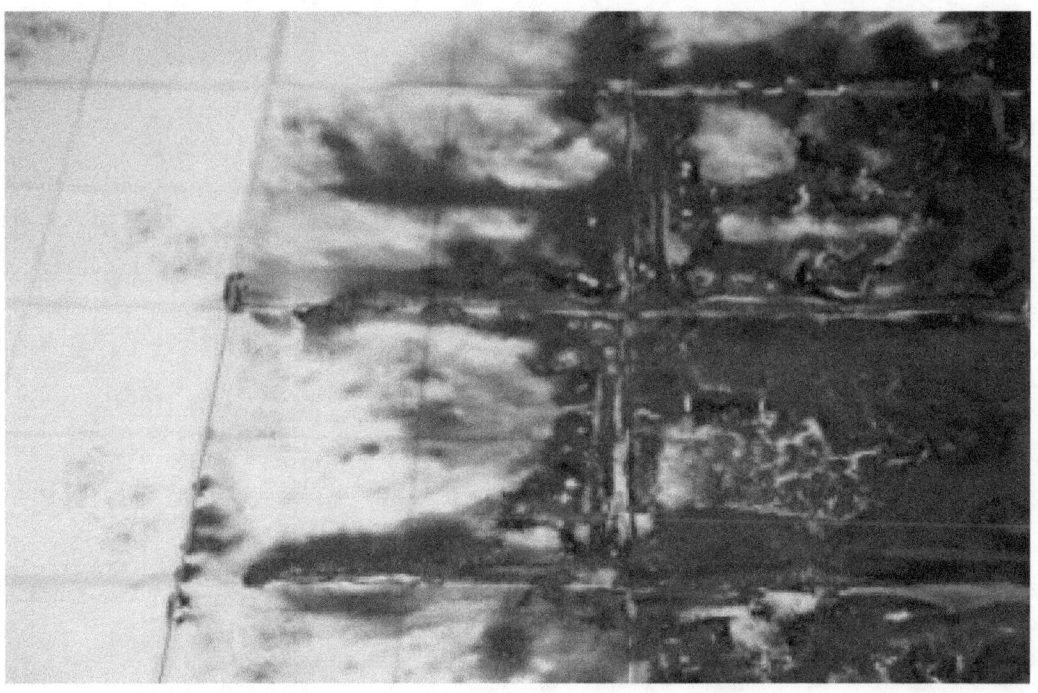

Figure 11. *Closeup of gasoline spill fire pattern on vinyl floor*

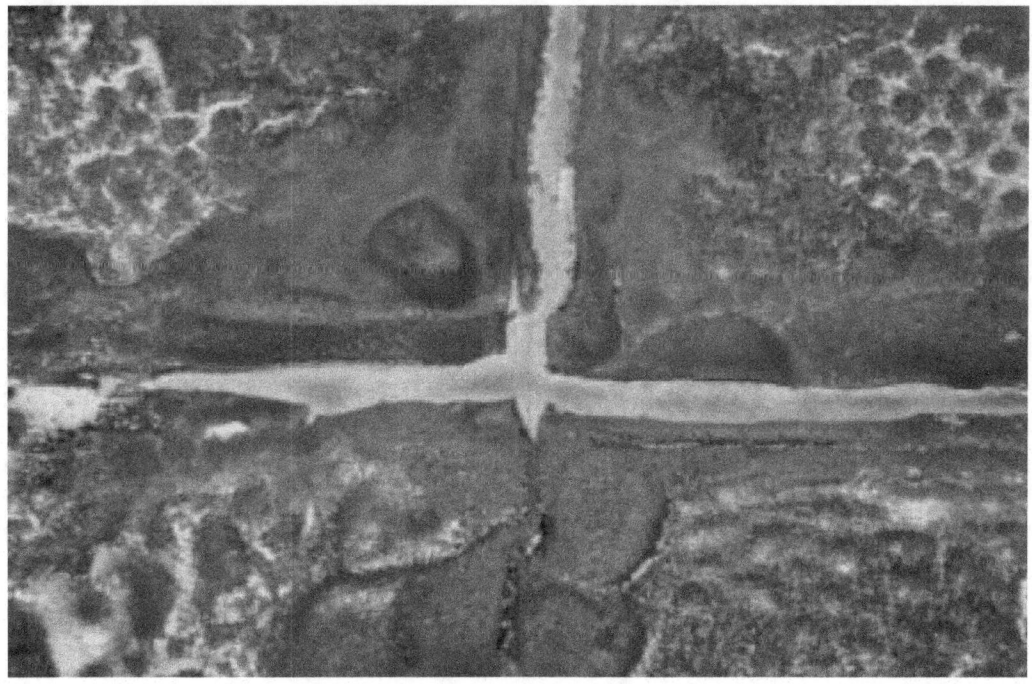

Figure 12. *Closeup of gasoline spill fire burn pattern on vinyl floor. Photo shows the retreat of the tiles at the intersections.*

Figure 13. *Vinyl tile removed after a 1,000 mL gasoline spill fire. Damage to the fiberboard is limited to the vinyl tile seam locations.*

Figure 14. *1,000 mL kerosene spill burn pattern*

Figure 15. *1,000 mL gasoline spill fire on carpet 1 at approximately 10 s*

Figure 16. *1,000 mL gasoline spill fire on carpet 1 at approximately 100 s*

Figure 17. *1,000 mL gasoline spill fire on carpet 2 at approximately 10 s*

Figure 18. *1,000 mL gasoline spill fire on carpet 2 at approximately 100 s*

Figure 19. *Closeup view of 250 mL gasoline fire on carpet 1*

Figure 20. *Closeup view of 250 mL gasoline fire on carpet 2*

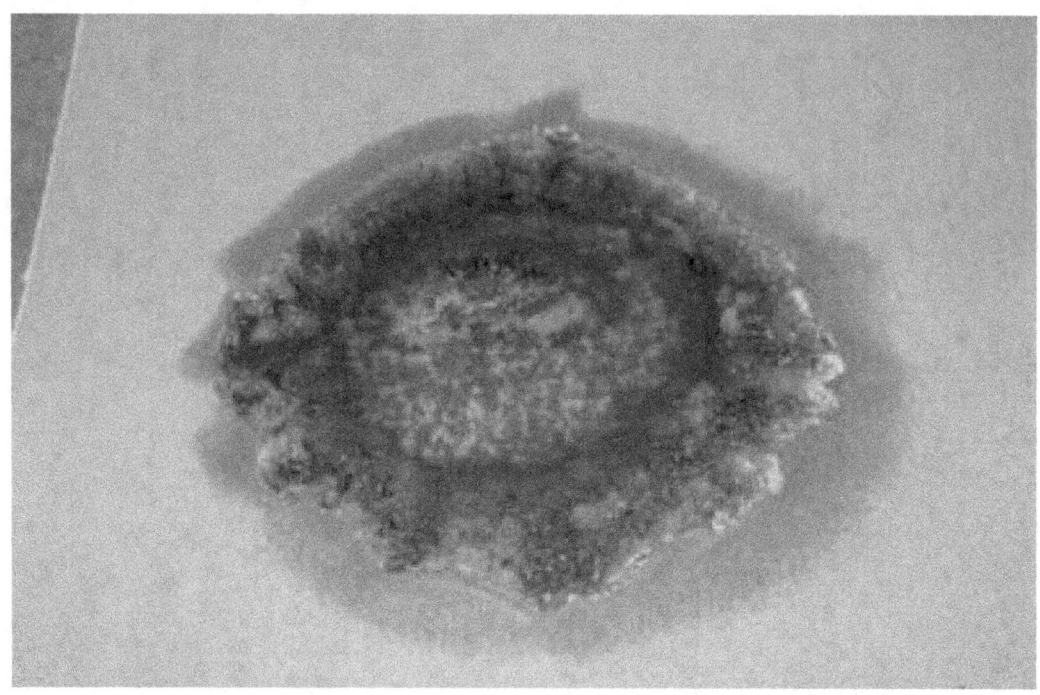

Figure 21. *Doughnut burn pattern on carpet 1. 250 mL gasoline fire extinguished at approximately 146 s with CO_2.*

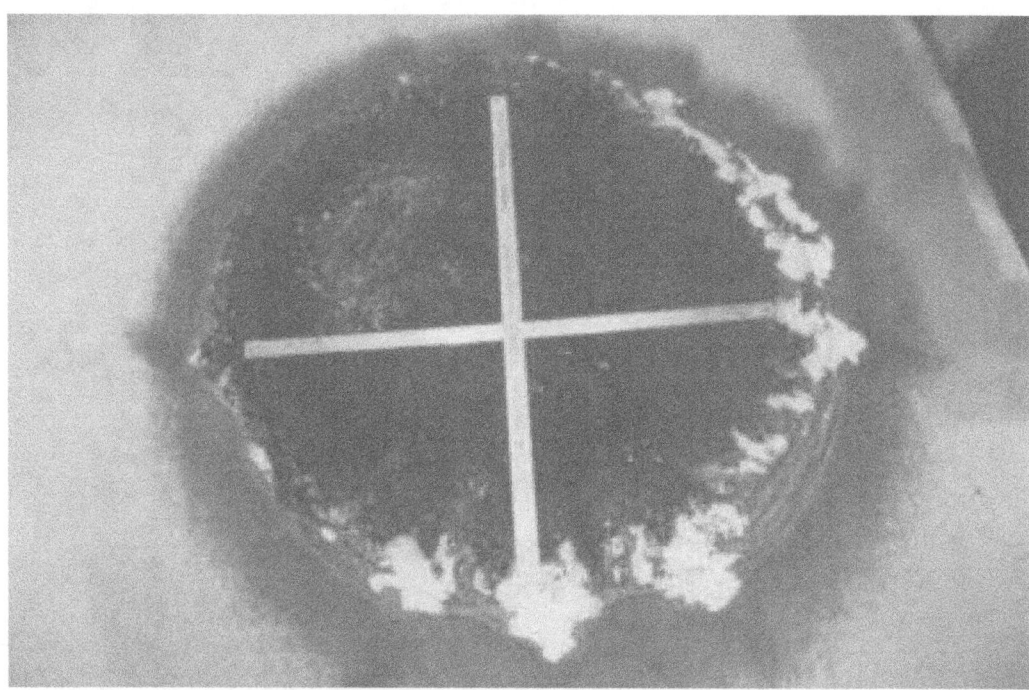

Figure 22. *Doughnut burn pattern on carpet 1. 1,000 mL gasoline fire extinguished at approximately 111 s with CO_2.*

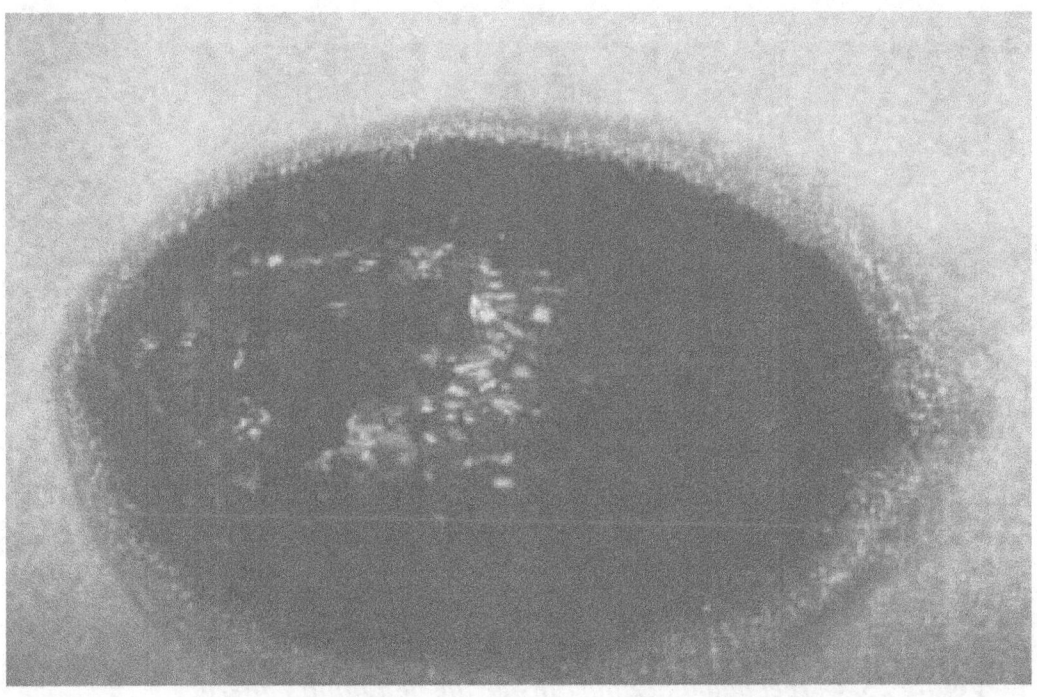

Figure 23. *Doughnut burn pattern on carpet 2. 250 mL gasoline fire extinguished at approximately 171 s with CO_2. Exposed padding can be seen in the center and toward the left side of the pattern.*

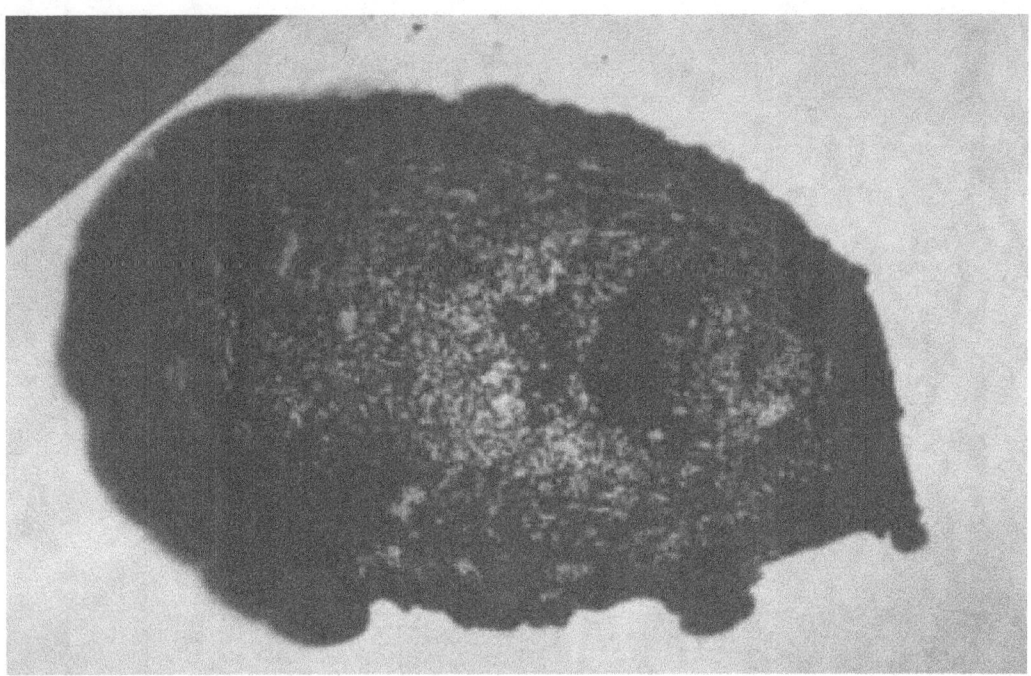

Figure 24. *Doughnut burn pattern on carpet 2. 1,000 mL gasoline fire extinguished at approximately 1,763 s (≈30 min) with CO_2.*

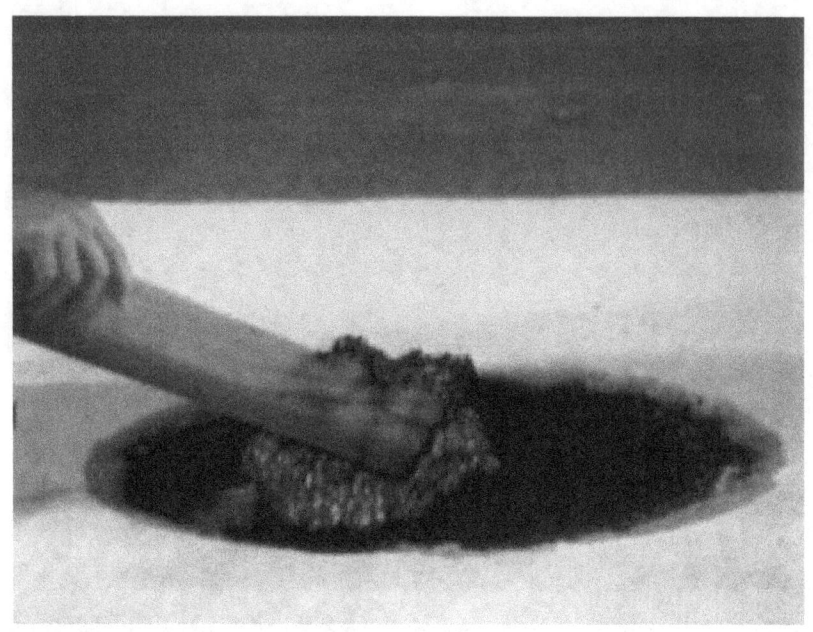

Figure 25. *Carpet padding intact inside the doughnut pattern. 500 mL gasoline spill fire on carpet 2. Fire was extinguished at approximately 234 s with CO_2.*

Figure 26. *1,000 mL gasoline spill fire on carpet 2 at approximately 600 s. This fire yielded the pattern shown in figure 24.*

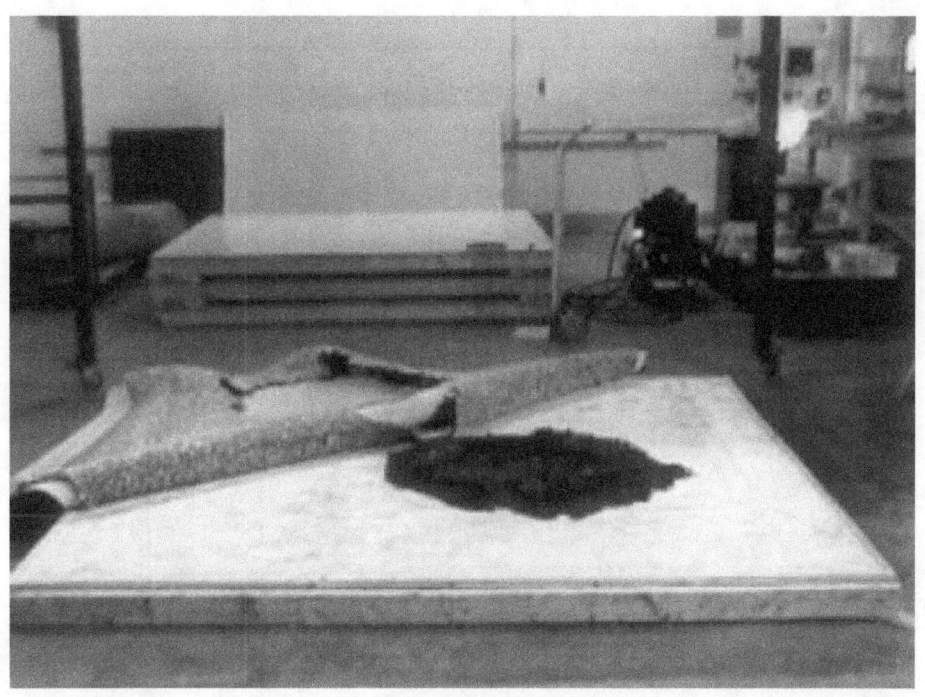

Figure 27. *Carpet and padding removed from floor leaving doughnut pattern behind. Results shown for 250 mL gasoline spill on carpet 1 extinguished with CO_2 after approximately 213 s of burning.*

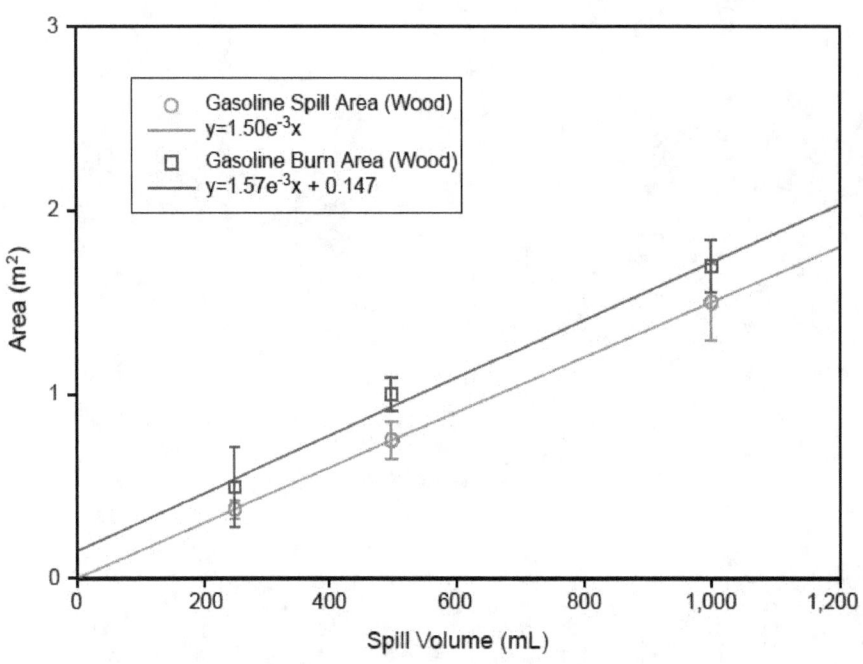

Figure 28. *Gasoline spill and burn pattern areas on wood parquet floors*

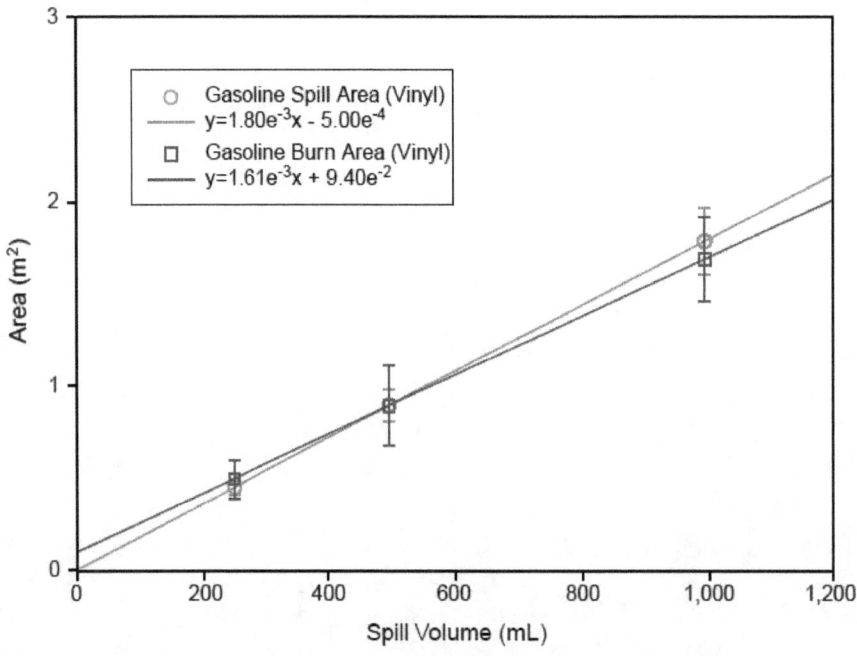

Figure 29. *Gasoline spill and burn pattern areas on vinyl tile floors*

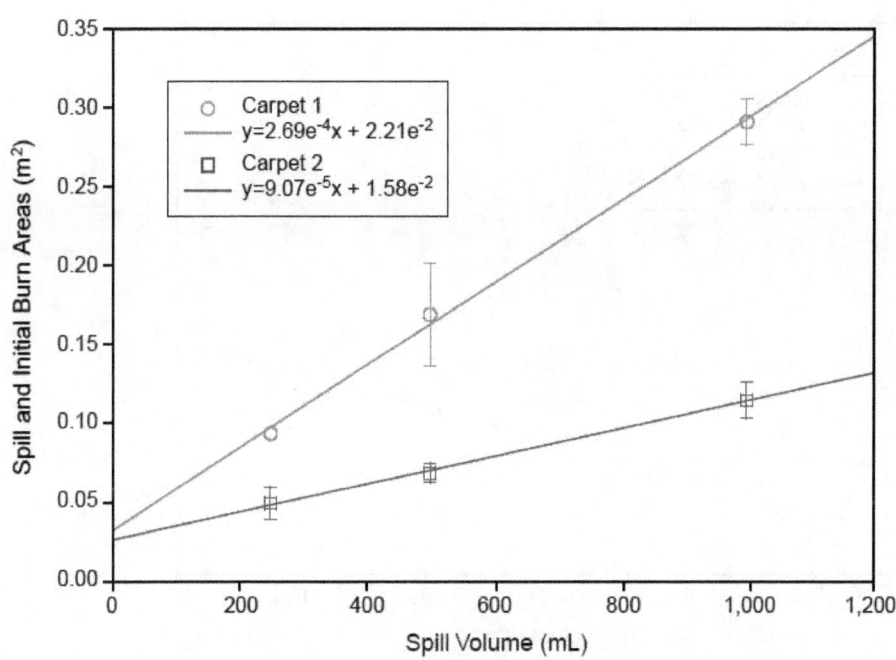

Figure 30. *Gasoline spill and initial burn areas on carpet-covered floors*

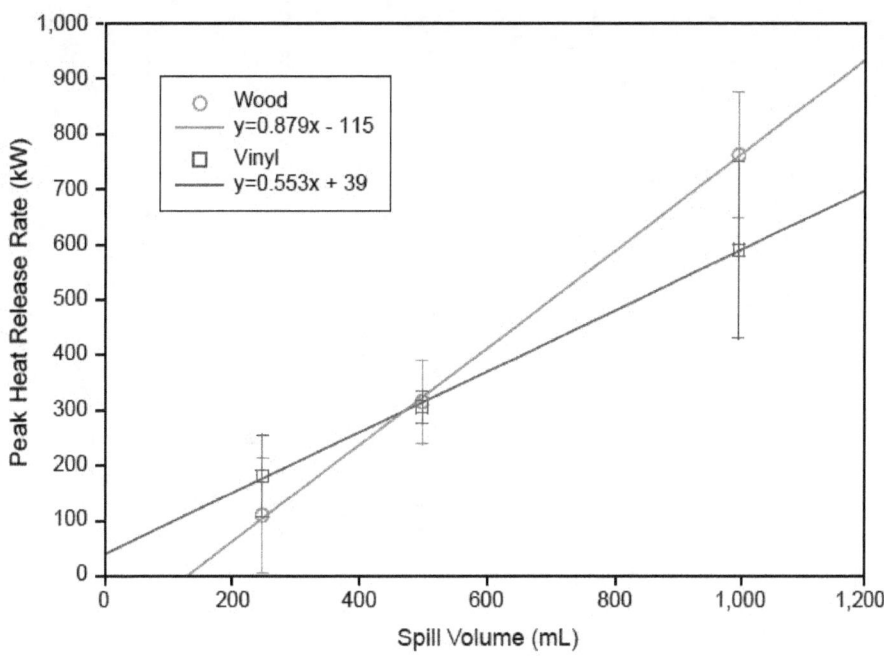

Figure 31. *Peak heat release rates for gasoline spills on wood parquet and vinyl tile floors*

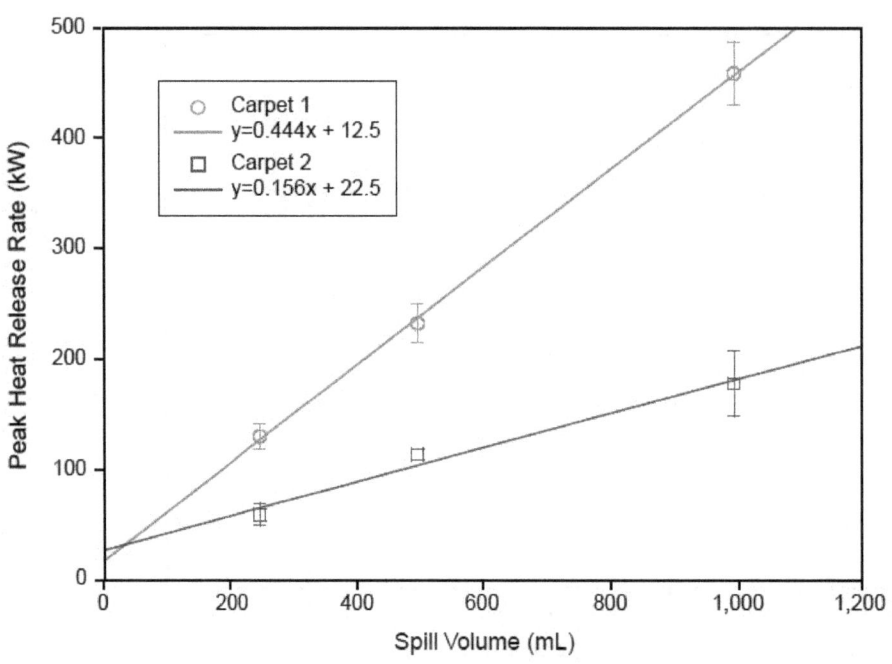

Figure 32. *Peak heat release rates for gasoline spills on carpet-covered floors*

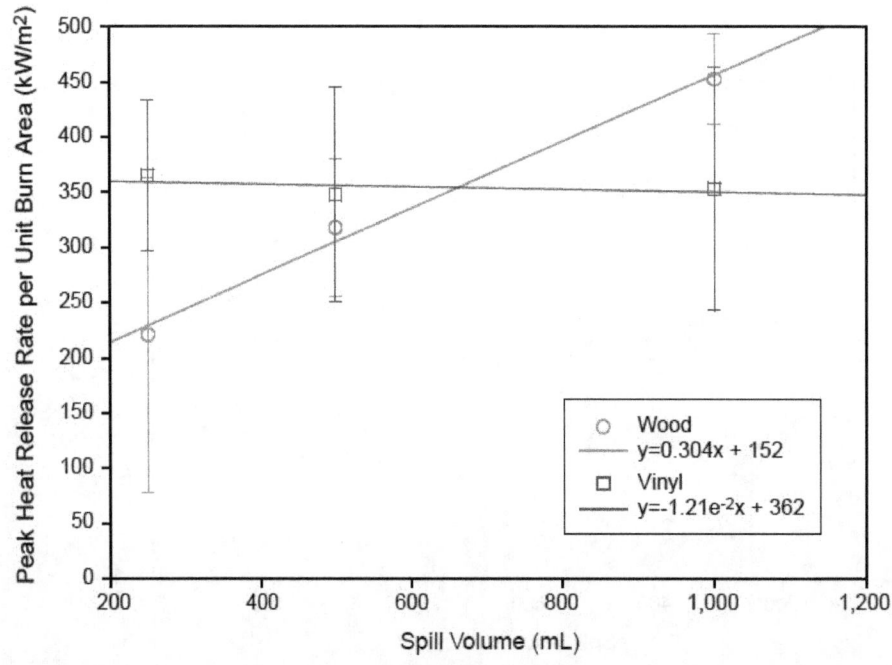

Figure 33. *Average peak heat release rate per unit area for gasoline spill fires on wood parquet and vinyl tile floors*

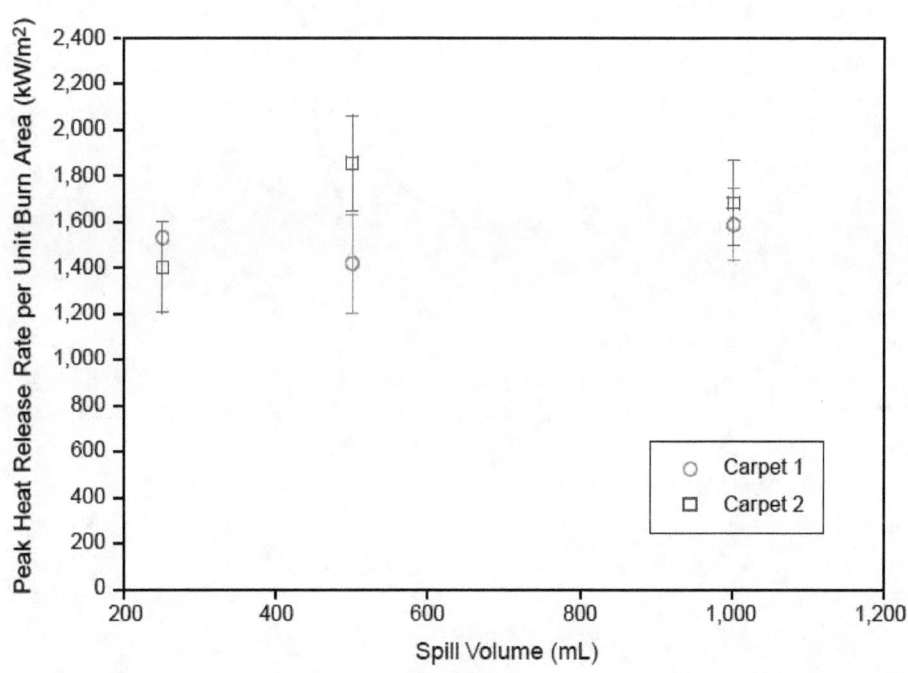

Figure 34. *Average peak heat release rate per unit area for gasoline spill fires on carpeted floors*

APPENDIX A—HEAT RELEASE RATES

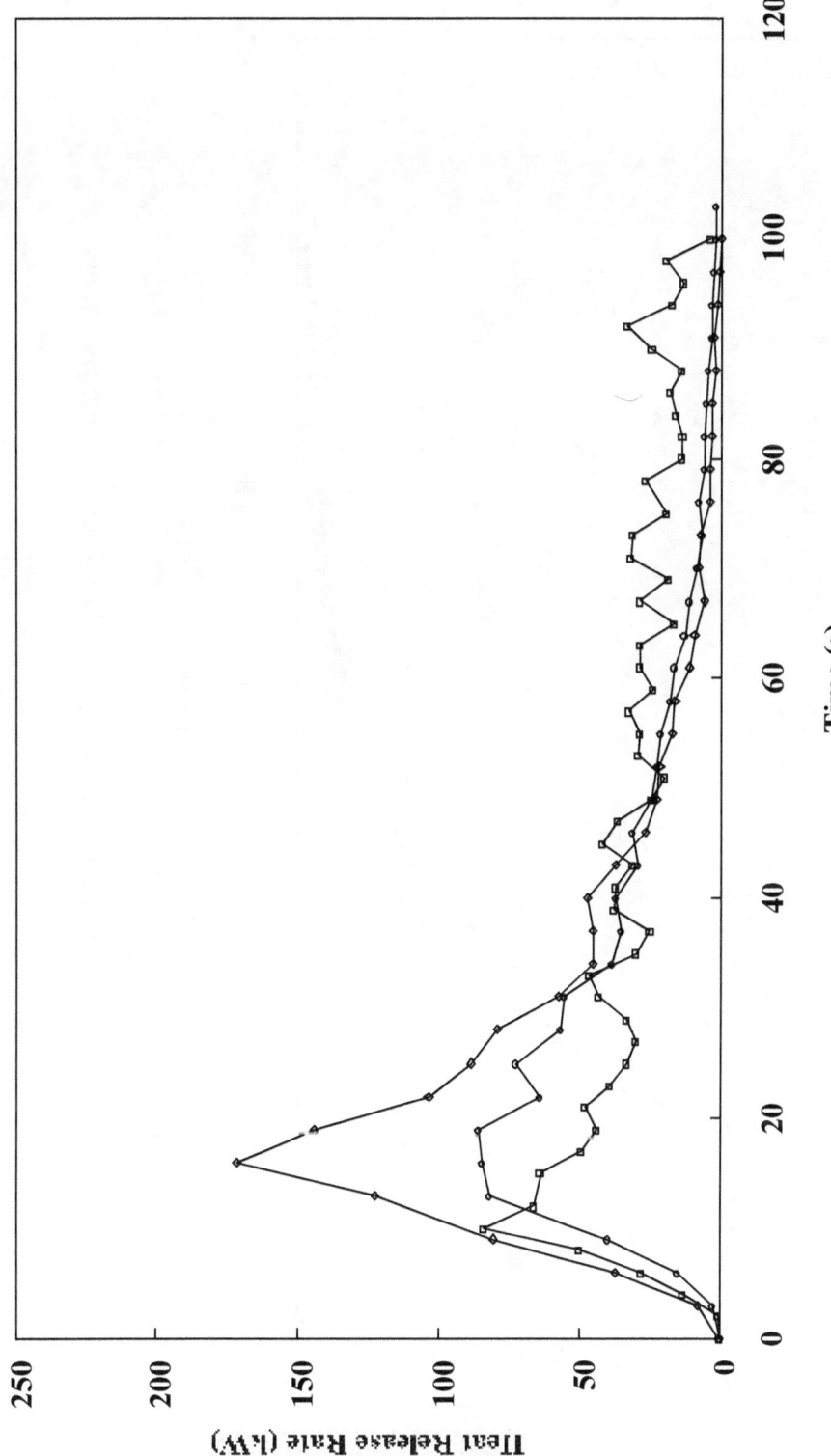

Figure A1. Heat release rates of 250 mL gasoline spill fires on wood parquet floors

33

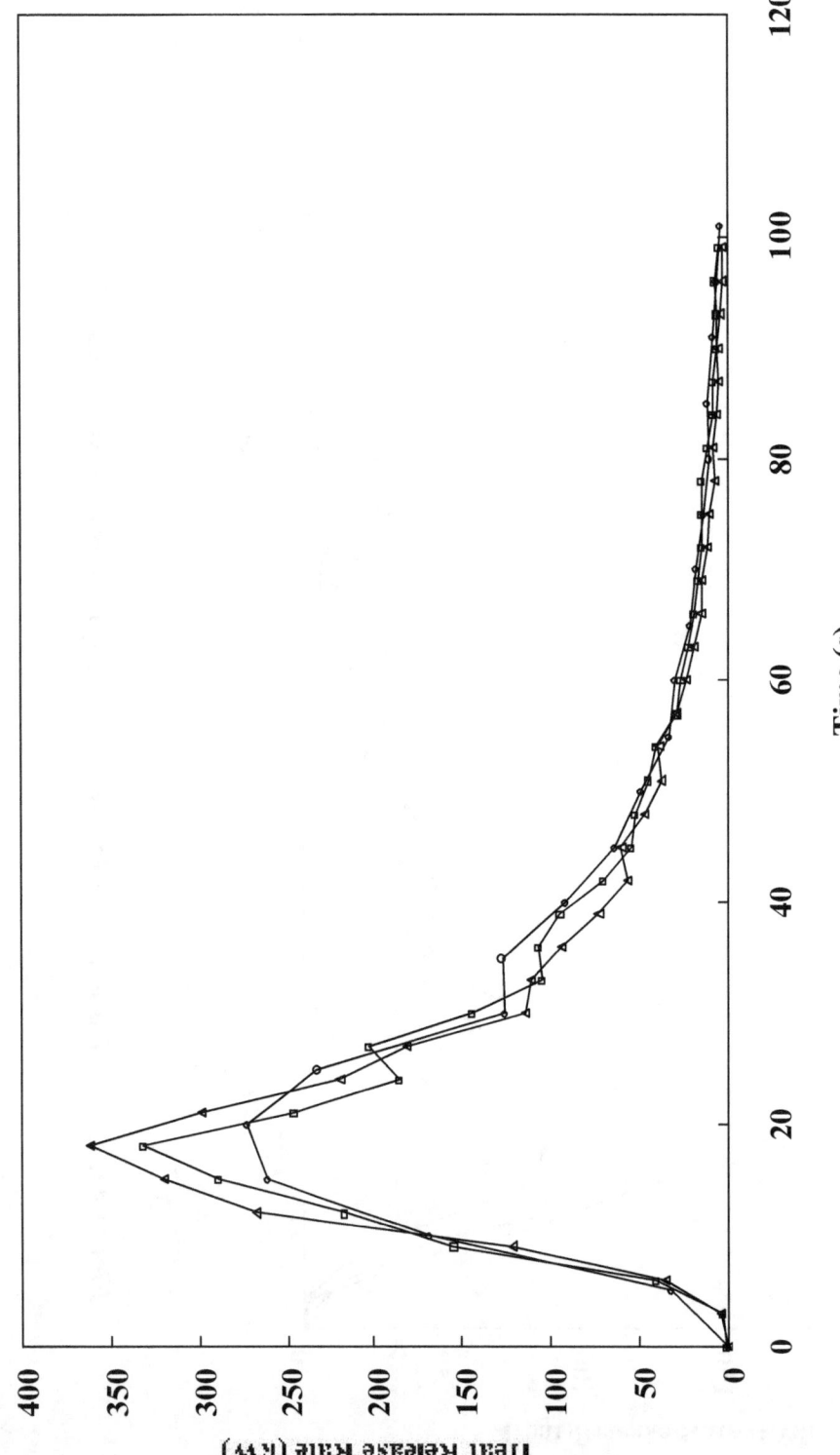

Figure A2. Heat release rates of 500 mL gasoline spill fires on wood parquet floors

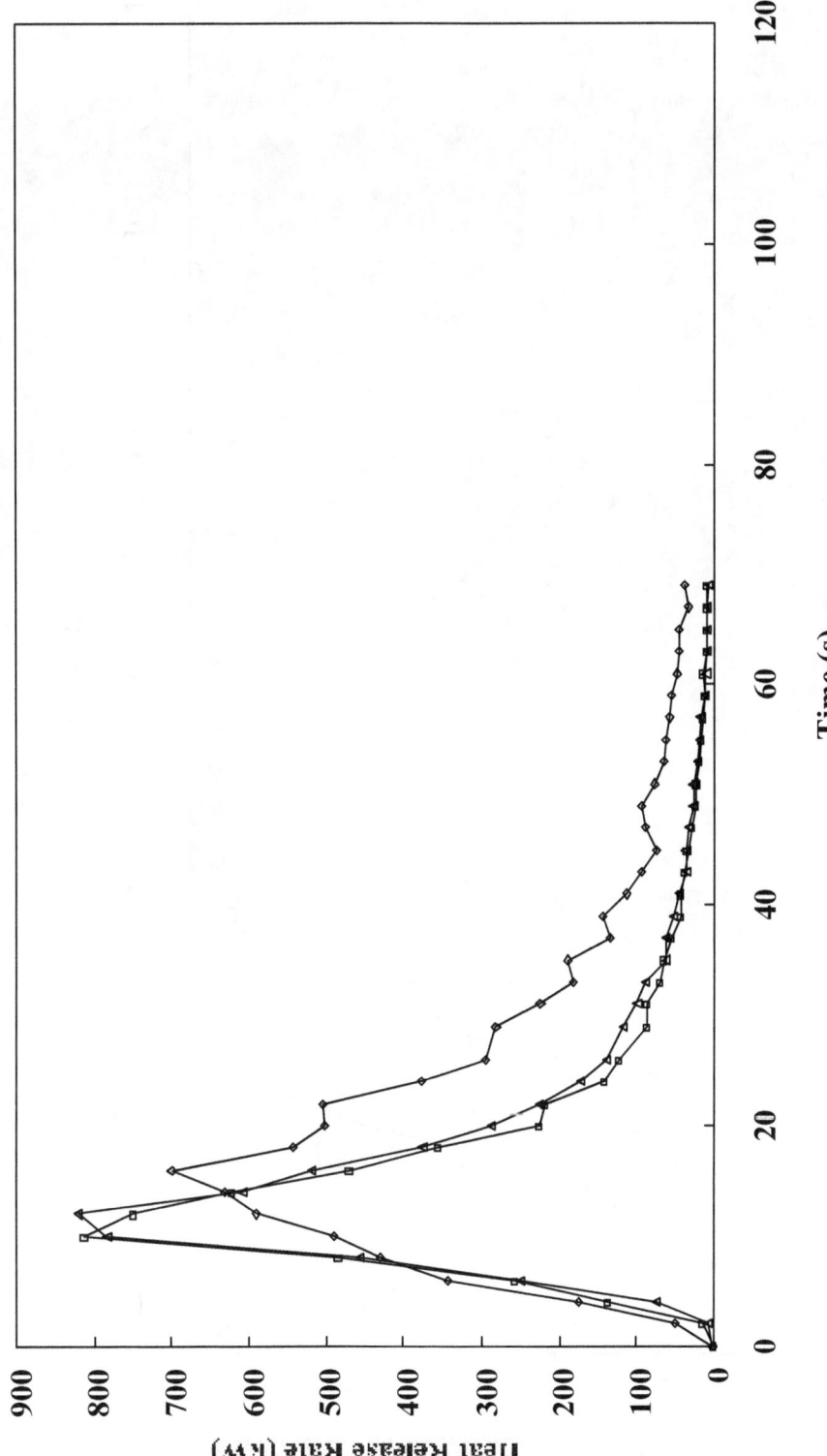

Figure A3. Heat release rates of 1000 mL gasoline spill fires on wood parquet floors

35

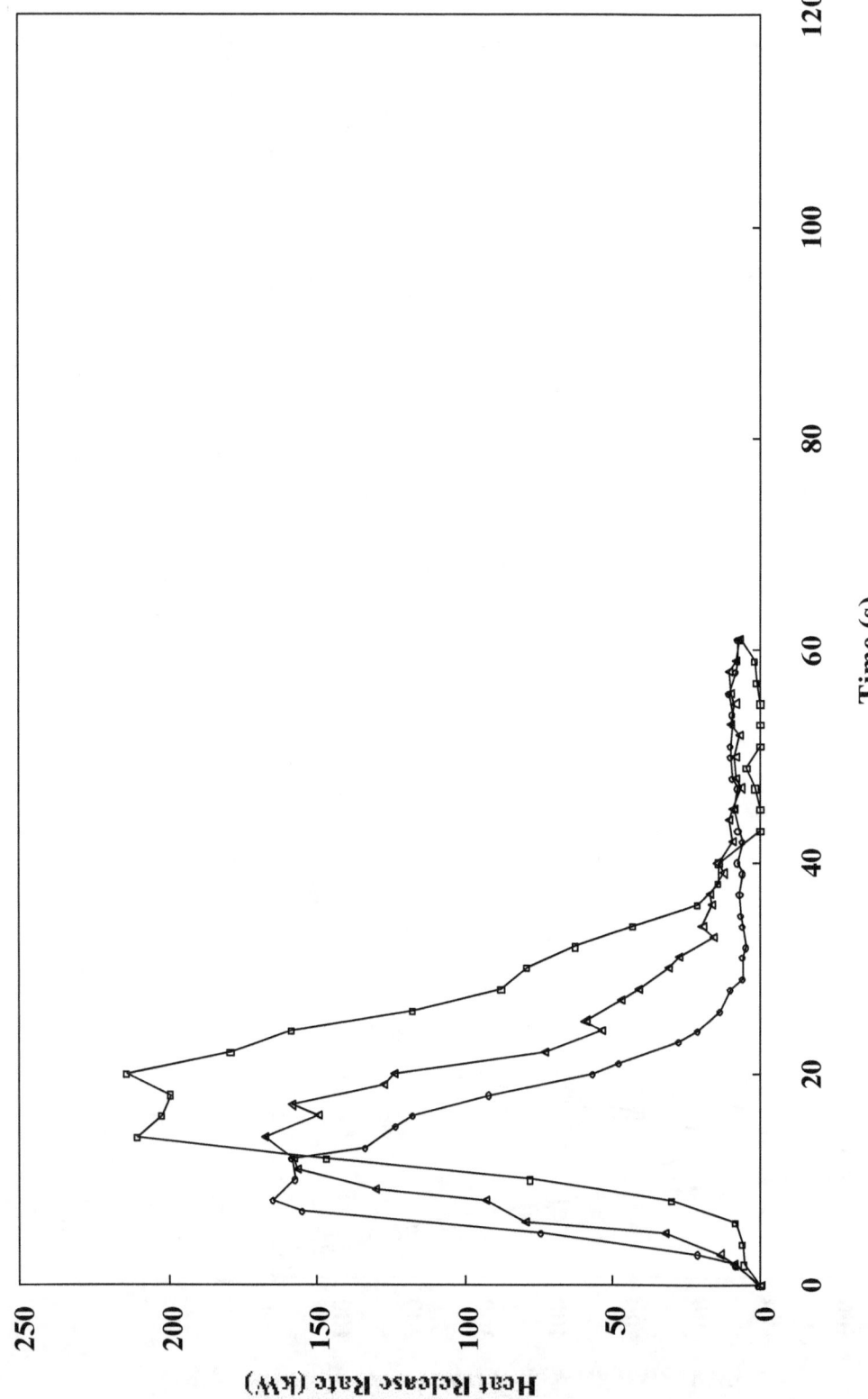

Figure A4. Heat release rates of 250 mL gasoline spill fires on vinyl tile flooring

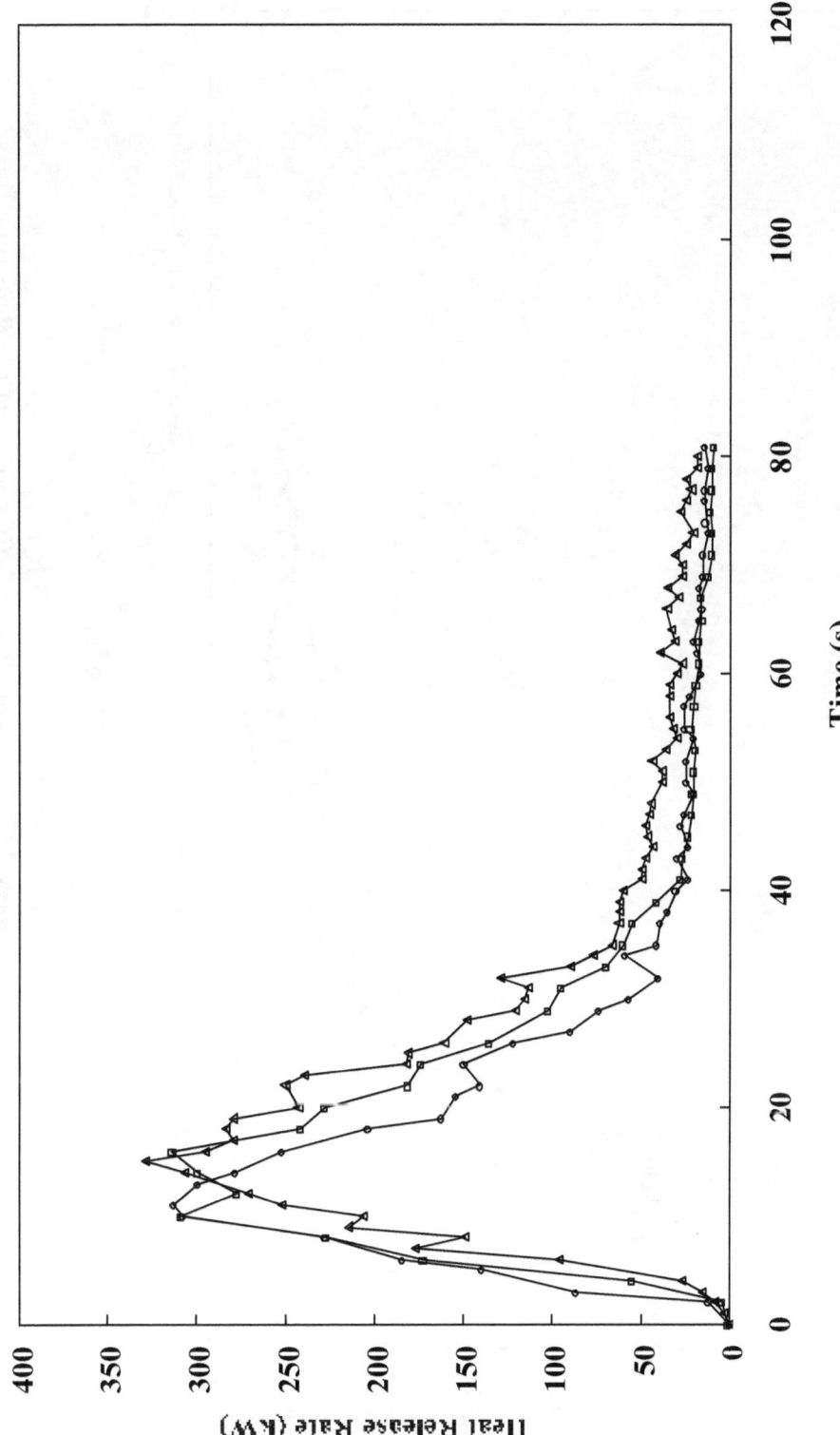

Figure A5. Heat release rates of 500 mL gasoline spill fires on vinyl tile flooring

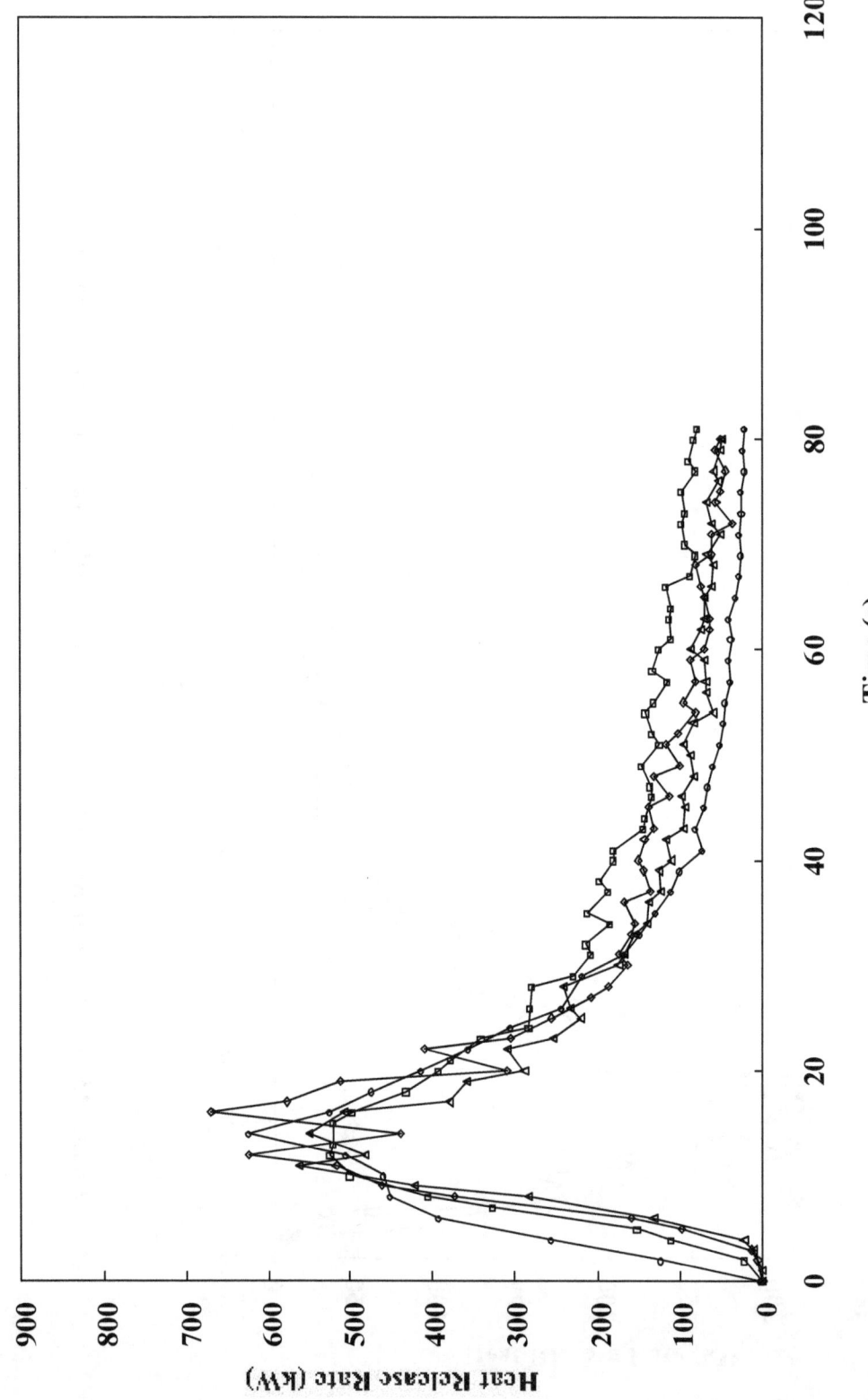

Figure A6. Heat release rates of 1000 mL gasoline spill fires on vinyl tile flooring

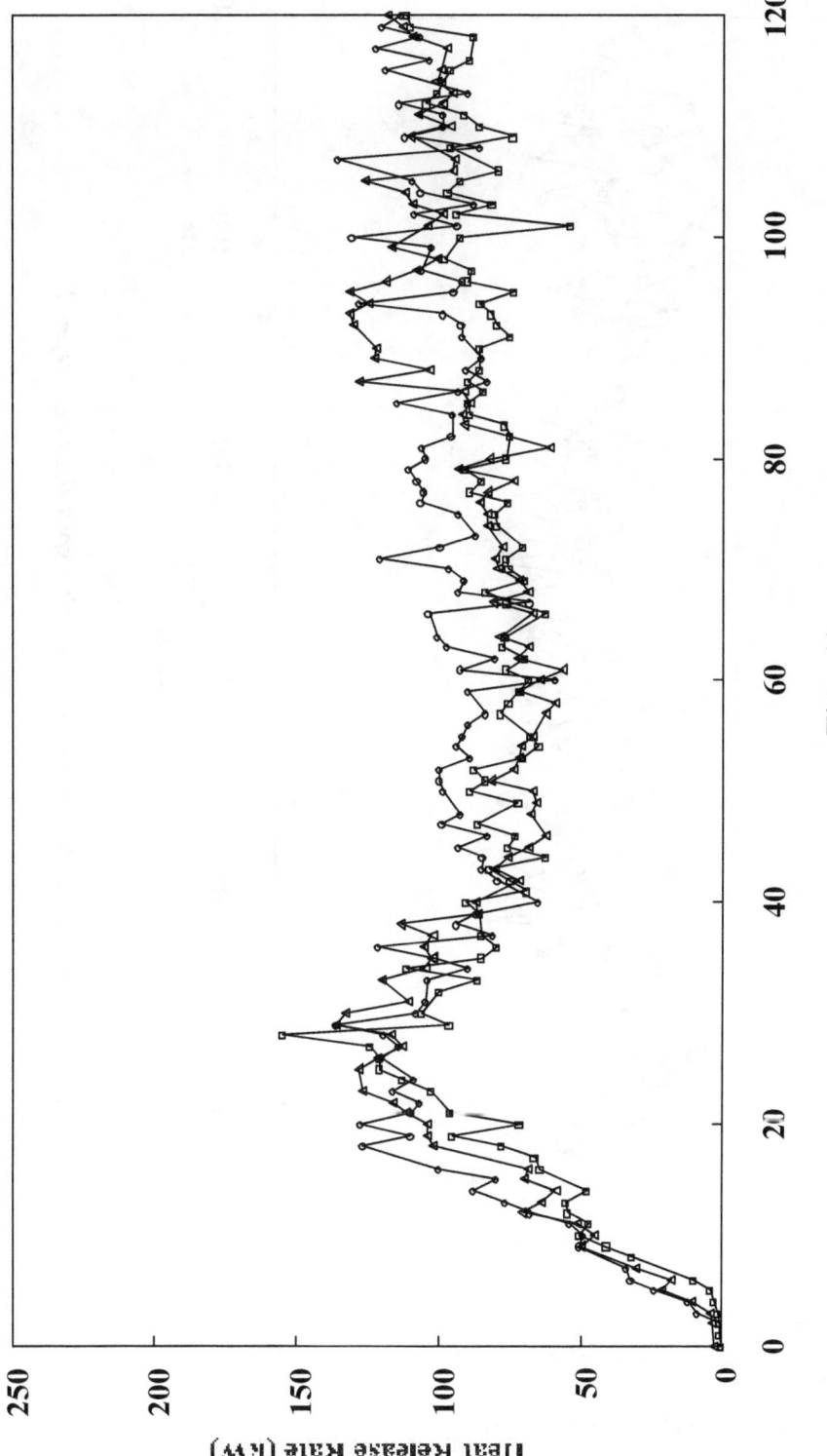

Figure A7. Heat release rates of 250 mL gasoline spill fires on carpet 1

39

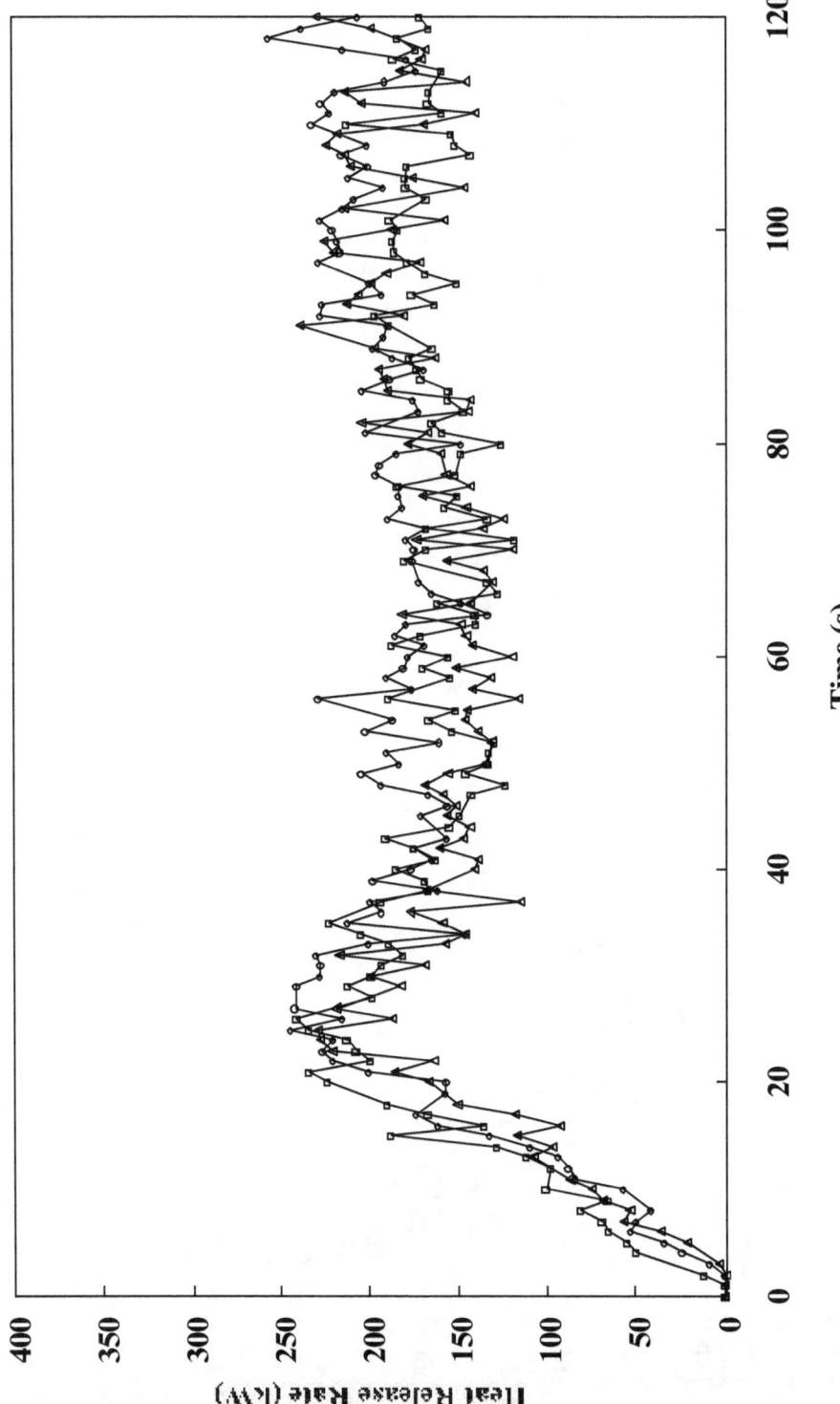

Figure A8. Heat release rates of 500 mL gasoline spill fires on carpet 1

40

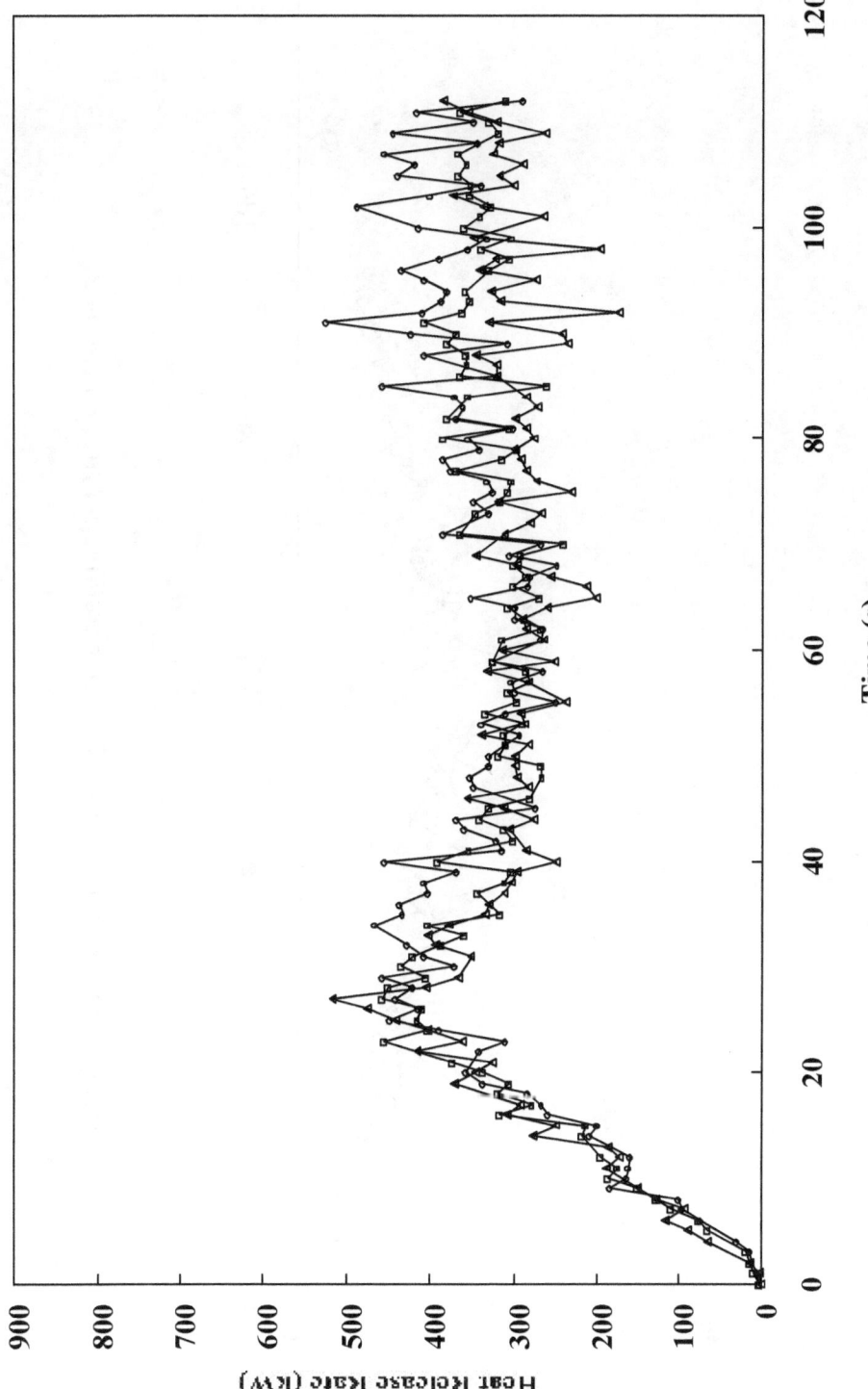

Figure A9. Heat release rates of 1000 mL gasoline spill fires on carpet 1

41

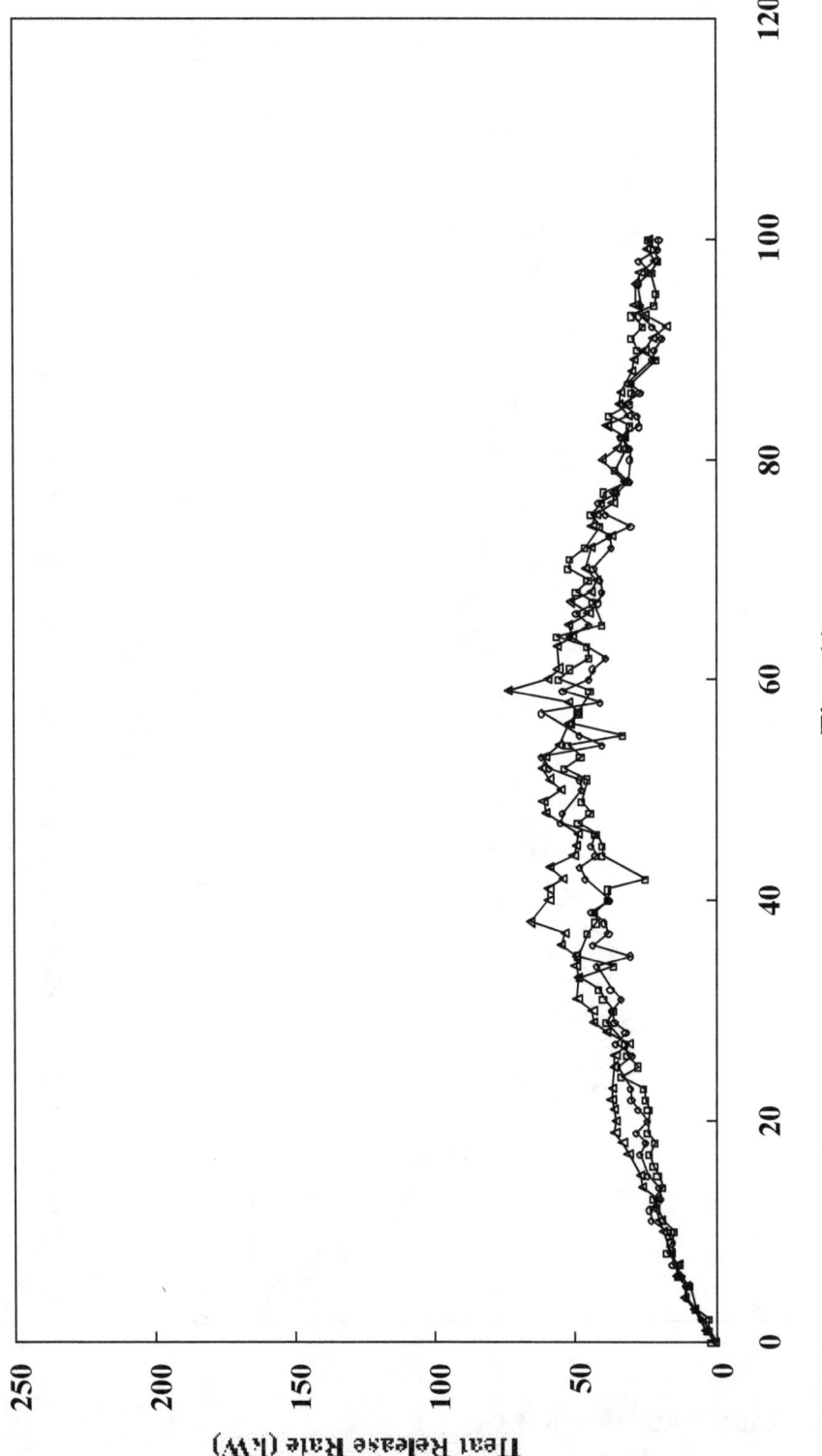

Figure A10. Heat release rates of 250 mL gasoline spill fires on carpet 2

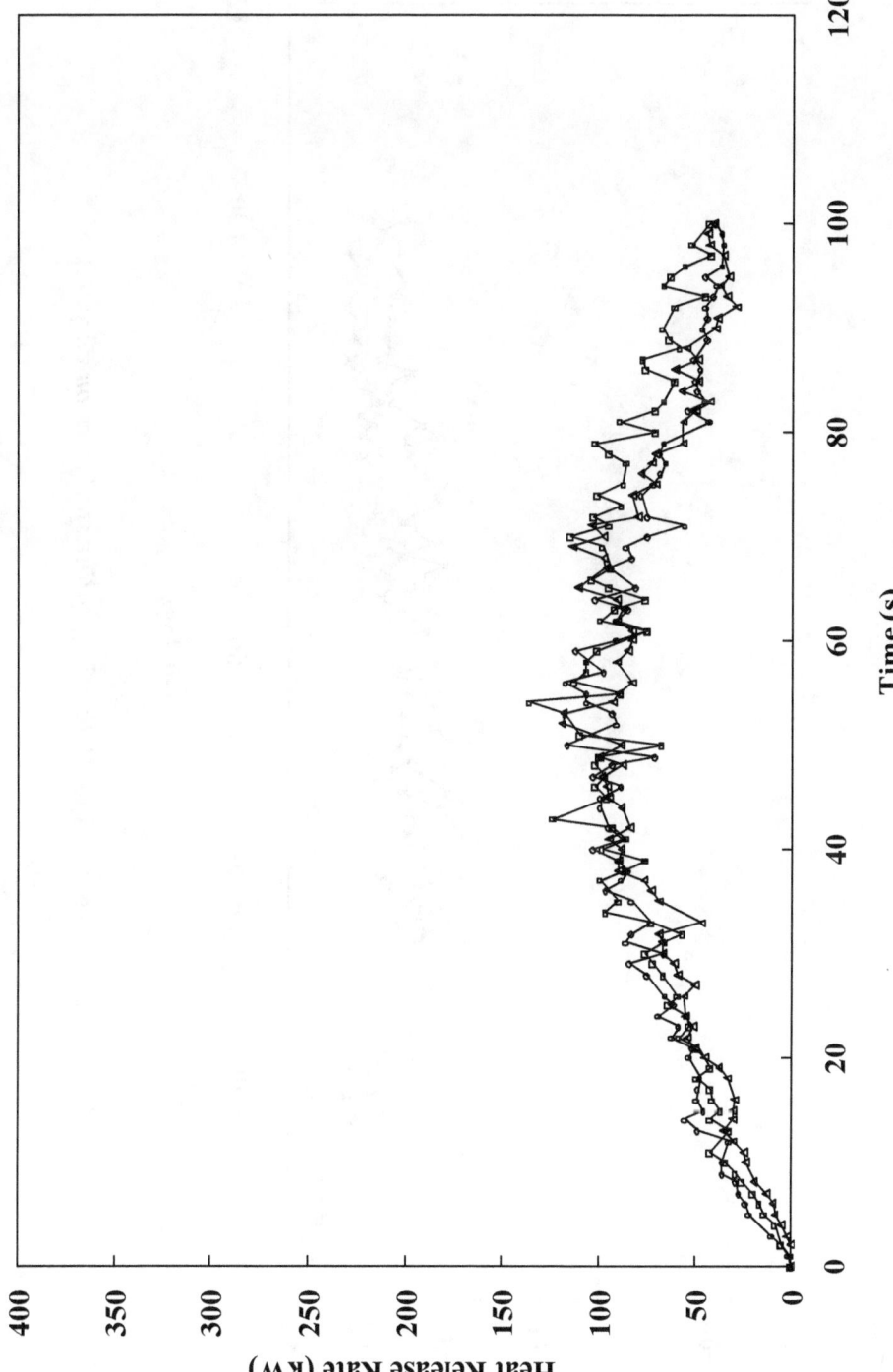

Figure A11. Heat release rates of 500 mL gasoline spill fires on carpet 2

43

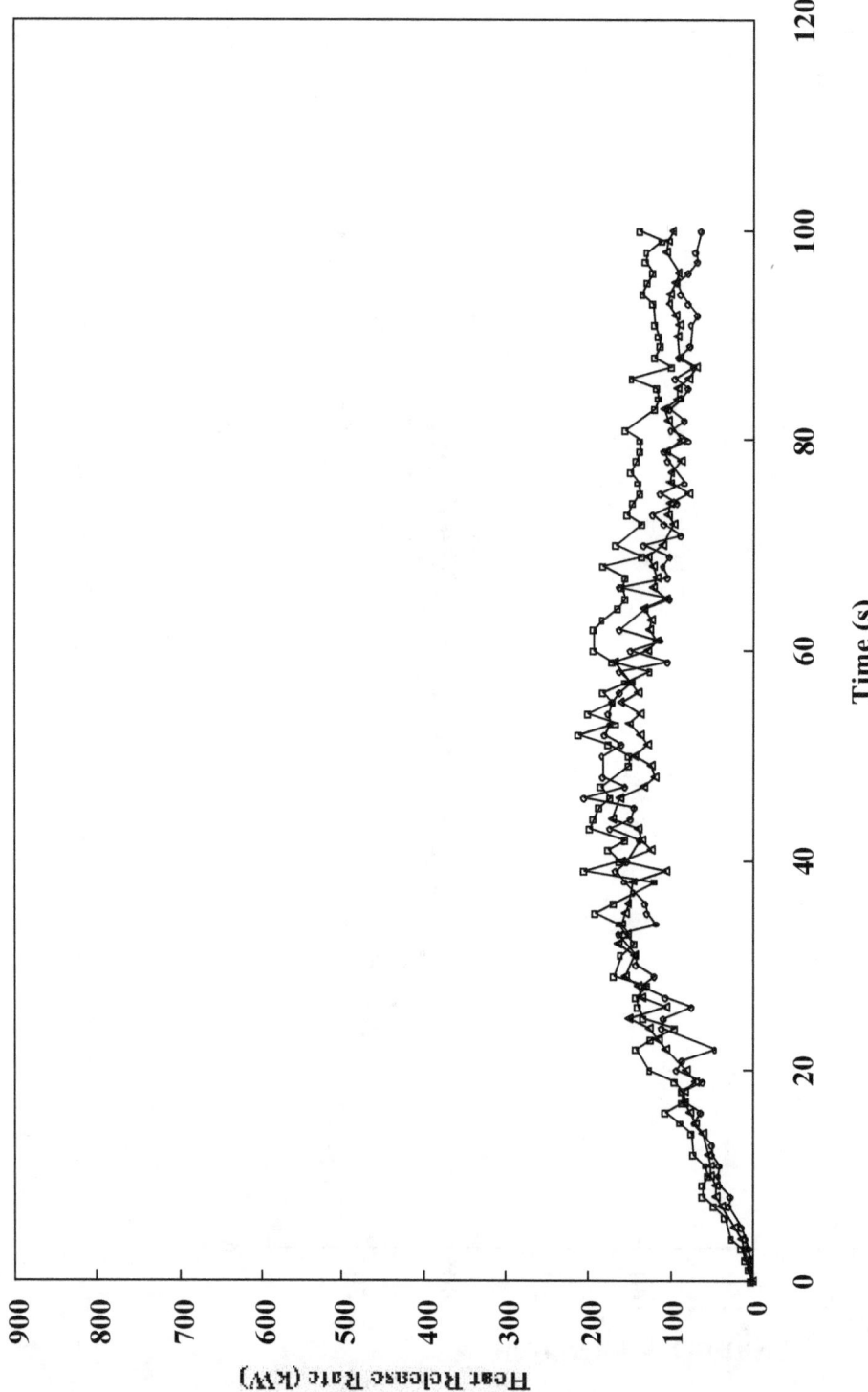

Figure A12. Heat release rates of 1000 mL gasoline spill fires on carpet 2

www.ingramcontent.com/pod-product-compliance
Lightning Source LLC
Chambersburg PA
CBHW080609180526
45168CB00007B/2837